MW00986884

How to Market a University

How to Market a University

Building Value in a Competitive Environment

Teresa M. Flannery

Johns Hopkins University Press · *Baltimore*

Johns Hopkins University Press
2715 North Charles Street
Baltimore, Maryland 21218-4363
www.press.jhu.edu

Library of Congress Cataloging-in-Publication Data

Names: Flannery, Teresa M., 1961- author.
Title: How to market a university : building value in a competitive
    environment / Teresa M. Flannery.
Description: Baltimore : Johns Hopkins University Press, [2021] | Series: Higher
    ed leadership essentials | Includes bibliographical references and index.
Identifiers: LCCN 2020018968 | ISBN 9781421440347 (paperback) |
    ISBN 9781421440354 (ebook)
Subjects: LCSH: Education, Higher—Marketing. | Universities and
    colleges—Administration.
Classification: LCC LB2342.82 .F53 2021 | DDC 378.1/01—dc23
LC record available at https://lccn.loc.gov/2020018968

A catalog record for this book is available from the British Library.

*Special discounts are available for bulk purchases of this book. For more information,
please contact Special Sales at specialsales@press.jhu.edu.*

Johns Hopkins University Press uses environmentally friendly book materials,
including recycled text paper that is composed of at least 30 percent post-consumer
waste, whenever possible.

To Brian Blair, whose love and support make audacious plans possible

To Helen Flannery Sylvester, whose fierce determination and persistence are my inspiration

To fabulous colleagues, whose creativity and courage have always been the keys to my success

Contents

Preface

When Greg Britton, Editorial Director of Johns Hopkins University Press, asked to meet me, I was not prepared for his proposition. The Press had a successful series for higher education leaders, with practical books that represented the how-tos of the Academy. They wanted a book on higher education marketing, which leaders were starting to recognize as an area of growing strategic importance. Britton had asked several leaders in higher education marketing who should write the book. He said they had all given him my name. If he thought flattery would work, well, he was right. I was thrilled. And then terrified.

With my dissertation more than 20 years in the rearview mirror, and with professional writing experiences limited (weekly crisis communication notwithstanding) to an article here and a chapter there, the prospect of generating 60,000 words to capture the state of the profession I love in an accessible format for leaders was daunting. Yet I understood the privilege and responsibility of representing the significance of this work at a time that couldn't be more challenging in higher education. The call to serve was irresistible.

Colleagues who have occupied the same role in higher education that I have, that of chief marketing and communication officer, know that it is a 24/7 role. It leaves little time for other pursuits, and the schedule is wildly unpredictable. Despite my best attempts as a part-time author, I was not making the necessary progress. But I was determined not to let this opportunity pass, so in June 2019 I left my position on the executive team at American University and dove headlong into a self-funded sabbatical.

A creature of organizations and teams, I knew I had to provide myself with structure, discipline, and interactions to complete the task. I polled my faculty friends, asking them how they managed to stay focused and on track. From the best public libraries in the area to how to manage my daily schedule, including writing, organizing, and exercising, their advice was crucial, but the best counsel I received made this endeavor a real joy. Professor James Thurber, an eminent scholar and prolific writer, suggested that I send a paragraph description for each chapter to a colleague with expertise in the subject and then set up an hour-long call to discuss it. "Record the call, and when you are finished, the chapter will virtually write itself," said Jim. The chance to knock around ideas and gather the thoughts of others gave this extrovert the energy and interactions needed to make the task a little less solitary, and it sharpened my thinking. These "book whisperers," as I came to call them, along with an aggressive schedule—a chapter draft due to my research assistant every two weeks—kept the ideas flowing and the fingers flying. I highly recommend Thurber's method to new authors, and I have newfound appreciation for the diligence and dedication required in service of scholarship.

As I wrote, another book on the JHU Press higher ed list was selling like hotcakes. Nathan Grawe's *Demographics and the Demand for Higher Education* provided a daunting perspective on the decade ahead, and higher education leaders were describing it as a frightening read. One president, Britton told me, stopped him in the middle of downtown Washington and told him Grawe's book had kept him up all night. It was in that context that this book came to life. Its subject grew even more urgent as the manuscript was in editing, with a global pandemic and the economic impact accelerating the threats to enrollment, revenue, and the basic business model.

The decade ahead may be among the most challenging times ever faced in higher education, and presidents, provosts, and trustees are searching for strategies that will help their institutions prepare to survive and thrive. Smart leaders who recognize that marketing is a strategic function, one that builds not only reputation but revenue and other value, will be in the best position to organize and help their institutions to thrive. What looks like the greatest challenge of the decade ahead could be leaders' greatest opportunity, and there is no time to waste. I hope this book serves as the guide that they need to organize, resource, and measure marketing efforts that will build value, sustain their institutions, and maybe even help them sleep through the night.

Acknowledgments

I realize that a book is no solitary achievement. If it takes a village to raise a child, it takes a network to produce a book that will stand the scrutiny of colleagues and satisfy the expectations of readers.

In this instance, that network has a crucial component that makes the rest hum—and that would be my research assistant, Angela Polec. A higher education chief marketing officer and professional in her own right, Angela is more accurately described as my thought partner, and this work is better for her involvement in countless ways. I came to know Angela through work on her own dissertation, when she was introduced to me by her dissertation advisor, a former graduate assistant of mine. I think that makes Angela my professional descendant, and if the future of higher education marketing is in hands such as hers, we're going to be in fine shape. I'm immensely grateful for her intellectual nudges and her familiarity with both the current and the seminal literature in our field, as well as her facility with endnotes and style guidelines. If it weren't for Angela, I'd still be lost somewhere in Microsoft Word help, struggling to figure out formatting.

If Angela is my professional descendant, then I am a product of professional mentors who have shaped me as a higher education leader and marketing professional. Linda Clement (University of Maryland) has been my mentor and friend for forty years. Her integrity, standards for quality, and curiosity are among the most powerful forces shaping my professionalism. President Emeritus Neil Kerwin gave me my first opportunity to serve in executive leadership at American University, and his mentorship and guidance have prepared me for leadership at even greater levels of impact. I've learned from some of the founding fathers of higher education marketing, including Larry Lauer (Texas Christian University), Tom Hayes (Xavier University), and Bob Sevier (Stamats), among others, men whose work ties directly to mine. Countless colleagues and team members at both the University of Maryland and American University shaped the exemplary marketing referenced periodically in this book. Board members and leaders at both institutions were demanding, courageous, and supportive, which allowed us to produce some of the most successful and groundbreaking work in higher education marketing. All these colleagues and mentors constitute my network and have made me the leader I am today.

Every powerful network includes supercomputing capacity, and in the case of this book that would be the brilliant strategists I've dubbed my "book whisperers," who hopped on a call with me to talk through a chapter before I started writing. These talented leaders are among the most respected practitioners in higher education marketing and communication: Elizabeth Johnson (SimpsonScarborough), Bill Faust (Ologie), Rob Moore (CASE, Lipman Hearne), and Bill Walker (currently at UMass Dartmouth, and his professional trail has included successful stints at Brandeis, the University of Arizona, CASE, RPI, Rutgers, Dartmouth, and William & Mary). I'm indebted to each of them for the gift of their time and the intellectual property shared to help our field mature and improve. Other leaders, including Peter Barber (Lipman Hearne) and Michael Eicher (Ohio State University), provided important ideas during professional exchanges that also informed my thinking about this work.

I'm grateful to presidents who shared their perspectives as they were going through the process of developing or launching a brand strategy. Karl Einolf (Indiana Tech), Troy Hammond (North Central College), and Margaret Drugovich (Hartwick College) shared accounts of their experiences, which I know will be helpful to their peers.

Last, but not least, my network includes a backbone—the large and extended Flannery family, including my husband, Brian Blair; our adult children, Kevin, Kerry, Brigitta, and Ashton; my mother, Helen; and my brothers, Dennis, Dan, John, and Patrick, and their families, all of whom have been on this journey with me. Their love and continued support keep me grounded.

If most networks back up and store their important data in the cloud, then my network includes important cloud-based support as well. We lost my dad thirty years ago, but somewhere up there beyond the clouds is a man whose love of learning and innovation was passed on to his only daughter at a very young age. As an adult, my summer vacations included buying two copies of the latest novel by our favorite author of spy thrillers, one for him and one for me. We'd pummel each other with questions and commentary at the end of each chapter and race to see who could finish first. I'd dearly love to put this book in Paul Flannery's hands, but I am certain it is already backed up in the cloud.

How to Market a University

Introduction

Why Marketing?

We just finished all of this change program, we have repositioned ourselves, and working under that strategic plan, it's time to rebrand the institution.

—Troy Hammond, president, North Central College

A key function of a university leader is to responsibly manage institutional assets. Often, we think of these assets in terms of financial and physical resources—endowments, reserves, operating funds, property, equipment, and physical plant. Less often, we think of the equity in an institution's brand, one of its most valuable assets. It isn't recognized as such, perhaps because it isn't an item on the balance sheet. Yet we know, instinctively, that awareness of the institution, the strength of its reputation, and its ability to draw in and engage students, supporters, funders, and partners have a direct influence on our strategic goals and financial well-being. Just as leaders carefully consider an investment strategy and choose a chief financial officer and investment manager to steward and build investment assets, they also need to effectively organize and lead the strategic integrated management of their brand. In order to effectively communicate an institution's value, one must first identify and build that value. This book addresses how to do that well in the context of higher education, where the competition is fierce and the need to differentiate is necessary to survive and thrive.

The pressures to stand out, successfully compete, and meet an institution's goals have never been more acute. In a period of declining public support,[1] a shrinking pipeline of traditional college-bound students, and a steady rise in tuition and discount rates—and in the wake of a devastating global pandemic that is likely to permanently alter the higher education landscape for years to come—leaders are under intense pressure to ensure steady or growing enrollments, cultivate greater philanthropic support, grow research funding, and diversify revenue streams, all while strengthening institutional reputation.

College and university leaders have been slow to recognize that strategic integrated marketing is beneficial for meeting all of these goals, but in recent years marketing has come of age in higher education. In a 2013 survey of chief executives at four-year institutions, presidents ranked strengthening the institution's reputation as second only to a balanced budget among measures of presidential success.[2] Recognition of the importance of this priority is shared by leaders of universities not only in the United States but also worldwide. Forces including globalization, changing educational funding in the United Kingdom, and immigration policies in the United States and Europe combined to draw international students and faculty toward Canada, Australia, the Middle East, and Asia, which have developed competitive global institutions and policies designed to attract them.

In 2017, the Council for the Advancement and Support of Education (CASE) convened a leadership symposium in which the leaders of ten of the world's leading universities had deep conversations about the top challenges and opportunities they faced. They all mentioned the primary importance of a compelling narrative to communicate clearly about the value and relevance of their institutions. Peter Mathieson, then president and vice-chancellor of the University of Hong Kong (and now principal and vice-chancellor of the University of Edinburgh), put the use of modern brand marketing tools at the top of his list: "Defining what it is that your own institution stands for, what you really believe in, what is your niche, what are your strengths, what are your weaknesses. I think universities need to focus on our strengths." Mathieson suggested that effective use of these tools requires elevating a few clear strengths in the institutional narrative rather than diluting it by trying to include everything. "We can't be excellent at everything."[3]

Anton Muscatelli, principal and vice-chancellor at the University of Glasgow, said that to achieve a genuinely distinctive status locally, nationally, and globally, "we have to ensure that what we do in the marketing area is absolutely central to our strategy lead. Marketing has to be part of the strategy, not just a tactical device to sell the university, which is sometimes how it is interpreted."[4] Muscatelli's observation is critical to the central premise of this book, which is that marketing strategy is, at its core, institutional strategy, encompassing decisions not just about communication or promotion but also about choices with respect to programs, experiences, pricing, or modes of delivery. These choices define a distinctive position in the market environment, differentiating the institution from direct competitors.

Presidents, provosts, and board members are keenly interested in what it takes to succeed in marketing, and their questions about how to begin or improve inevitably include the following: How should marketing efforts be staffed and organized in a college or university? How much should be invested? How does one know when the strategy is working? What measures does one use to track progress? Each leader sees the need from their own distinct perspective, but all share an interest in understanding how marketing should be done, who should lead it, what it will cost, and how to measure results.

This book seeks to address the interests of all those leaders and starts with the perspectives they bring to the practice of marketing. It seeks also to assist chief marketing officers (CMOs) in understanding and effectively addressing the needs and interests of these leaders, whose support they need to succeed. I borrow liberally from my own experiences with leaders at two institutions that engaged in some of the most well-known early successes in higher education marketing; and I reference leaders at other US and global institutions and marketing leaders who are setting the pace for professional marketing in higher education.

The Purpose of Marketing, through the Lens of Various Leadership Roles

The chief executive officers (CEOs), who for the purposes of this book are referred to as presidents (alternatively called chancellors or, outside the United States, vice-chancellors), are among those who hold the widest view of their institutions and the landscape within which they compete. They interact regularly not only with members of the institutional community—including students, faculty, staff, alumni, and parents—but also with donors and prospects, foundation leaders, peers and competitors, business and community leaders, government officials, and members of the media. It is through this wide lens that presidents form their views of the purpose and broad outcomes that marketing and communication efforts should achieve and the gaps that must be addressed.

Under pressure from their boards to elevate the profile of their institutions, presidents want to ensure that the stories of their colleges and universities are told in a manner that effectively promotes perceptions of excellence, quality, and value. They expect the mission, vision, and values of their institutions, and often key aspects of their strategic plans, to be expressed through inspirational and consistent messaging in all marketing to many constituencies. "Without being arrogant or prideful, we want to make sure that the outside world understands what we think is important. It's kind of interesting to be in a marketplace as competitive as this one—it really does keep you on your toes," said Neil Kerwin, then president of American University.[5]

Presidents understand that if they are to stand out from competitors, they must distinguish their institution from those in their competitor set, yet most academic leaders I've met are more comfortable listing the myriad ways they are *similar* to other institutions, especially those they aspire to be like. Resisting this instinct and working to find and articulate what is special or different is an important foundation of marketing.

It is difficult to be unique in higher education. Only a few institutions, such as Berea College in Kentucky or Olin College of Engineering in Massachusetts, truly come close to that kind of distinction. However, differentiation in mission, offerings, or message, especially among those with whom an institution competes head to head, is achievable, and it is key. As the authors of the Distinct project in the United Kingdom advised, "A distinctive identity is the vehicle which enables an organisation to achieve many of its strategic goals through being memorable, authentic, and clearly articulating what it has to offer to the people that are important to it."[6]

That's why I appreciated the instincts of Dan Mote, who served as president of the University of Maryland during a period of rapid reputational rise at the turn of the twenty-first century. He had a basic requirement for 30-second ads that aired as public service announcements during football and basketball games (a no-cost opportunity to broadcast to key stakeholder audiences messages valued at millions of dollars annually): no lab coats, no beakers, and no filtered beauty shots of the campus. "I did not want another typical university television spot," he said, alluding to clichéd images of students ambling across the campus and white-coated scientists in the lab. "The university is supposed to be a clever place. It's not supposed to be humdrum."[7] In short, he encouraged his marketing team to avoid what all the other public research universities were doing, to stand out, to be memorable. He was a champion of courageous differentiation, and his instincts allowed Maryland to do some of the most distinctive early work in higher education marketing—work that made it stand out from competitors.

Some leaders see marketing primarily as delivery of one-way communication (let us tell you what we want you to know) and fail to see it as a two-way exchange, with goals that go beyond developing awareness and achieving recognition. In mature marketing efforts, leaders realize that the goal of promotion is to engage key stakeholders with a compelling offer that builds on their awareness of the institution to cultivate relationships that promote institutional support and loyalty. Moreover, leaders have begun to recognize that differentiation extends well beyond messaging. A strategy that differentiates the institution from competitors might highlight distinctive programs or services, the means by which they are accessed or delivered, or the price at which they are offered. These elements of the marketing mix represent all the ways that marketing strategy can advantageously set an institution apart in the marketplace.

There has never been a greater incentive in the higher education sector to differentiate. Presidents and boards are intensely aware of the need to build and diversify revenue at a time when net tuition revenue is flattening or in decline, routine tuition increases can no longer be sustained, and the pipeline of traditional college students is projected to essentially plateau until 2025, before it declines sharply in the late 2020s.[8] The demographic cliff that Nathan Grawe has forecast might seem like the leadership challenge of the next decade, but it also offers one of the greatest opportunities to adapt and thrive in a difficult environment.

In fact, the authors of *The College Stress Test* surmise that market consolidation among institutions in this decade will advantage the most prestigious institutions and those with "brand-name" recognition, while struggling institutions will have fewer options for changing the trajectory of their future, including pricing strategies that reduce market price (tuition resets) combined with comprehensive strategies to elevate the brand of the institution, as well as reengineering the first-year curriculum to improve retention. These choices not only reflect the aspects of the marketing mix that go well beyond promotion; they also reflect a mind-set that considers the needs of targeted student segments to make the institution more "student ready."[9]

Leaders who are the most sophisticated about the purpose of marketing make the direct connection between differentiating strategy and effective communication and engagement of constituents, motivating them to support the institution—the ultimate goal of marketing—through enrollment, philanthropy, state appropriations, and research funding. In other words, many interests of presidents are closely aligned with the purposes of effective marketing, even if previous experiences and backgrounds have provided a somewhat limited view of the purpose as tactical. Increasingly, leaders are recognizing that marketing strategy is institutional strategy, that these are two parts of a greater whole. It is the job of CMOs to recognize this alignment, to leverage leaders' interests, and to help them better understand marketing as a strategic investment that enhances their ability to meet many institutional goals—to build value through improved enrollment, philanthropy, and funding—as well as their ability to achieve greater brand equity (awareness, engagement, and loyalty), which is at the heart of reputation building.

Chief academic officers, who may hold the title of provost, dean of the college, or pro-vice-chancellor, share with presidents many of the same perspectives about the purposes of marketing, and given the background and experience of the majority of presidents, that's not surprising. However, since their focus is primarily on the central academic mission of the institution and responsibilities for academic leadership, their view of the role of marketing is sometimes narrower than those of presidents.

Provosts are keenly focused on academic reputation, though to the extent that they lead or influence major aspects of the student experience, they may be focused also on broader reputational issues. They consider faculty and students their primary stakeholders, and unless they spend a great share of their time with other groups, they may be less familiar with and attuned to the perspectives of staff, alumni, and external constituencies. That said, if admissions and enrollment functions are part of their portfolio, they are likely to have a strong interest in how their institutions are positioned and promoted, especially to prospective students and parents.

Chief academic officers often disdain and yet intensely scrutinize rankings of all sorts, especially those that include peer assessments, such as those appearing in *US News & World Report*. Peer review is an integral part of scholarship and tenure, and so peer attitudes are central to their sense of their own and other institutions. Hence, they may be particularly interested in marketing strategies that influence the views of their peers at similar institutions. Provosts share the tendency of presidents to put themselves in the company of other institutions rather than to differentiate themselves, which explains why so many institutions send the same kinds of materials with the same sort of messages to their peers just before the *US News* surveys hit their in-boxes.

Provosts often evaluate the relevance of positioning through the lens of faculty, which is sometimes aligned with but sometimes in direct contrast to what engages students. They expect that both learning and scholarship will be treated prominently and respectfully in messaging, often expressed in lengthy prose that achieves both precision and inclusion. *Academic excellence* is a phrase that many consider core to the institution's identity, and yet, could there be anything more descriptive of the aim of *most* colleges and universities and thus less differentiating?

Because of the power they wield, the experiences that have shaped their views, and the responsibilities they hold, chief academic officers offer some of the greatest challenges to development of marketing strategies that are differentiated, compelling, and relevant to a wide set of constituencies. And yet, the involvement and support of the provost and the faculty they lead are critical to building internal consensus and support for such strategies. Provosts who possess an appreciation for constituencies beyond faculty and students as well as for positioning strategies that are relevant to a wider set of audiences and that are intended to influence a number of institutional goals, are integral to success of marketing efforts.

If provosts lean more naturally toward marketing that appeals to internal audiences and influences other academics, board members, by contrast, lean toward changing perceptions beyond the institution and the academy—though trustees often share provosts' fascination with rankings. Board members hold great aspirations for their institutions and some of the greatest ambitions for marketing efforts. It is they who most often feel that the institution they serve is not sufficiently well known or recognized.

This view is reinforced in board members' interactions with external constituencies, who don't share the same familiarity with their institutions. Sometimes board members' aspirations are expressed in well-worn clichés, such as "our light is hidden under the proverbial bushel basket" or "our quality is the best-kept secret." Among the trustees most knowledgeable about the purpose of marketing are business leaders and politicians, who often provide some of the best counsel and insight, given their own professional expertise. Experienced trustees who understand the practice of professional marketing can support CMOs and help academic leaders appreciate the necessary scope of the effort, as well as the resources needed to change perceptions of image and reputation.

While trustees are interested in building the reputation of their institution, their primary responsibilities as fiduciaries drives their interest in building and diversifying revenue, as well as in appointing leaders with strong experience in financial and enrollment management and institutional positioning. A scan of any presidential search prospectus identifies these as among the most important and desirable capabilities of future leaders. Though they might not use the term *marketing*, boards increasingly seek leaders who can build these strategic marketing capacities within their institutions.

Board members I've worked with like to see and experience evidence of marketing at work. They notice how often they see people in their community wearing institutional apparel, the number of mentions in media they consume, the attitudes of colleagues and business partners hiring (or not hiring) graduates, the institutions those in their social circles support philanthropically, and the attitudes of parents and others related to applicants preparing to pursue a degree. These interests actually relate directly to common measures of brand strength, including licensing revenue, media mentions, employer attitudes and behaviors, giving rates, and perceptions of those who influence student applicants. So the instincts and insights of trustees, given their involvement both within and outside the institution, can be very important in supporting marketing efforts.

Board leaders provide the most valuable insight and input early in the development of all strategy. They are particularly useful in developing support for market research that leads to data-driven decisions about the focus of marketing efforts. Board members' interests should be primarily related to governance and oversight, not management responsibilities, which marketing plans clearly are. Trustees' greatest contributions are their insights about how to shape strategy, their support for the management decisions to fund and direct strategy, and their holding institution leaders accountable for the results related to those investments. Presidents and CMOs should avoid allowing trustees' interests to stray into tactical decisions about what to name the brand campaign, whether to put up a billboard, or how to devise a social media plan. That said, bringing trustees along for the journey and keeping them informed about research, strategy, budget, tactics, and results will bring valued insight to the task and support when it is most needed.

After all, no marketing or brand strategy is introduced with universal acclaim, especially in this day and age. In the age of social media, stakeholders can immediately react to any change in representation of the institution's identity, and they do. It is worth noting that few brands in any sector enjoy the lifelong loyalty that colleges and universities do. With the exception of professional sports teams, what other type of organization or company inspires people to plaster its name on their apparel, cars, laptops, credit cards, or even baby gear? Stakeholders consider their institution part of their personal identity. Influential members at the intersection of the internal and external communities—trustees—who participate in identifying the need for a marketing strategy and the process for shaping it and who understand the intended goals of marketing efforts are crucial in the early days of the launch. If they stand with institutional leaders, the strategy will have time to show its promise during the initial launch. If they don't have a stake, the early days of any new effort can be very difficult; over time, the lack of support can be crippling. There have been numerous instances when the lack of board support represented the demise of changes in logo, admissions marketing programs, and brand campaigns.[10]

The inaugural chair and vice-chair of the American University board of trustees's Communication Committee, both seasoned public relations professionals, were driving forces of board support for strategic integrated marketing and communication that would aim to increase brand awareness, improve the university's competitive position, protect the university during crises, and improve brand strength to positively influence enrollment and philanthropy. David Drobis, chair emeritus of Ketchum, and Margery Kraus, CEO and founder of APCO Worldwide, were staunch advocates for starting with market research to drive the strategy. They provided advice and input on the organizational structure and leadership, and their advocacy made a crucial difference, first in the adoption and then in the longevity of the university's first brand strategy.

As these examples demonstrate, board members' and other institutional leaders' perspectives on the purpose of marketing vary, ranging from less to more sophisticated. Leaders who want to succeed in the decade ahead will increasingly embrace marketing as a strategic function that helps them differentiate among competitors in a very challenging climate to engage stakeholders in relationships that support their institutions and build value, including revenue and reputation. To assist leaders in setting appropriate and achievable expectations, this book defines marketing, identifies its purposes in the context of higher education to build value, and describes the processes and tools needed to develop strategies that will move the needle.

A Question of Timing

If marketing strategy *is* institutional strategy, when should a process to develop or refresh the brand occur in relation to the development of overall institutional strategy? In preparation for writing this book, I spoke with several presidents, CMOs, and agency principals who are currently engaged in developing, launching, or refining college or university brand strategies. A surprising shift in attitudes emerged regarding the timing of brand development in relation to strategic planning: more leaders than I expected are beginning to recognize that brand strategy and institutional strategy are two parts of a greater whole. Data gathered from stakeholders inform the shaping of institutional strategy, starting with consideration of mission, vision, and values, continuing with analysis of competitors and identification of the strengths, weaknesses, opportunities, and threats that ultimately shape the institution's priorities in the form of strategic goals. These same inputs inform decisions about value proposition and positioning, which are at the root of brand strategy.

So which comes first, or should leaders develop or refine brand strategy at the same time as institutional strategy since the two depend on many of the same inputs and tools?

"Frankly, the two ought to be in lockstep with each other," says Karl Einolf, president of Indiana Tech, whose institution launched its new brand strategy in 2019.[11] That's quite a contrast to views in the early days of higher education marketing, when academic leaders wouldn't hear of allowing the needs of students and other stakeholders to influence what colleges and universities chose to do. But as competition has ramped up and pressure to increase revenue through means other than increasing tuition has grown, I've heard the earlier view expressed less often and support for Einolf's view expressed more frequently. In fact, this shift has created new options through firms that help institutions handle aspects of the two processes in tandem.

Elizabeth Johnson, chairman and partner of SimpsonScarborough, a marketing agency that works exclusively with higher education clients, thinks the processes should be linked from the beginning, at the research stage, and continue through the formation of institutional and brand strategy. From her perspective, integrating the two provides credibility and support for the brand process as a strategic initiative, one not to be easily written off as "just a marketing project."[12] Development of the brand strategy follows and is increasingly a direct outgrowth of the strategic planning process.

Troy Hammond, president of North Central College, in Naperville, Illinois, says the timing of his institution's process was quite deliberate, since the college had pursued an agenda of major change, which necessitated repositioning. As a new president, he first focused on completing a fundraising campaign and a facilities upgrade, then turned to a major curricular revision—with a new general education program and a shift in academic terms from quarters to semesters—change so significant that it required a whole new course catalog. The need for a fresh look at strategy was clear, so the college engaged in a year-and-a-half-long strategic planning process. One of the four pillars of the new plan is to make North Central a "college of destination" not just for students but also for faculty, staff, and others, who will see it as a place where they want to be enrolled, employed, and engaged. A whole host of tactics relate to branding and marketing in order for the institution to thrive in a more competitive environment. "This timing is not accidental," says Hammond. "It's exactly in sync. We just finished all of this change program, we have repositioned ourselves, and working under that strategic plan, it's time to rebrand the institution."[13]

Margaret L. Drugovich, president of Hartwick College, in Oneonta, New York, planned a board-approved sequence that started with market research conducted by The Art & Science Group, which yielded findings that four new strategic imperatives could powerfully motivate students to enroll and fully engage others to support the college in ways that were vital to its future. The board was apprised and kept current during the entire process of research and implementation planning. "I got the board to sign on early because I knew this would require their decision making and support," said Drugovich.[14]

In 2019-20, Hartwick's provost and vice-president of academic affairs led a year-long planning process called The Promise, in which members of the planning group, comprising representatives of all parts of the campus community, created a proposal for implementing the four strategic imperatives. Simultaneously, Drugovich astutely assessed the capacity of her marketing and communication team and decided to identify a marketing agency to participate in the planning process, so that the college's institutional strategy, essentially a repositioning, could be quickly and effectively expressed in a new brand while the institutional strategy was being developed and refined.

Karl Einolf at Indiana Tech advocates an institutional strategy based on what students want out of a college education and experience. "If we aren't offering the programs that students want, we aren't going to be in business for very long." For traditional students, "that might be the food in the dining hall, the amenities on campus, like WIFI outside on campus. You know, that might not be very important to me, but for them it's like having a dial tone on a phone. They want it in every nook and cranny on campus—with all five bars!" For adult students, "it's customer service, personal attention, engagement of online courses. Those are things that matter to students. . . . If we don't have those things, we need to address and deal with them." He suggests that an assessment of stakeholders' needs and expectations yields an understanding of both gaps and strengths that can be addressed or reinforced in strategic goals. Further, in areas where his institution is excelling, "we need to be able to communicate effectively about what's good and distinctive at Indiana Tech."[15]

Leaders who are open to considering the synergies of both processes welcome the opportunity to work on them together. For Einolf, it made sense to take on strategic planning and branding together:

> I saw the need to do both. It became obvious that we needed to do work on the brand assessment and strategic plan at the same time. Doing the research helped to form a strong plan. That information was really helpful for us as we thought about our future. It just gave us a better sense of what we needed to be working on as we worked to improve Indiana Tech.
>
> We knew as we developed the brand strategy that we needed to identify ways that we communicate those things important to our strategic goals. And one of the goals was creating a clear and consistent brand.
>
> It was just sort of a natural fit and one informed the other. The initial research among our constituencies about what we were known for and what the market's perception of us informed our planning process. Once we had our planning process, our strategic goals helped shaped the message in our brand strategy.[16]

Peter Barber, executive vice-president of Lipman Hearne, an integrated marketing and communication firm that works with higher education and nonprofit institutions, says this emergent thinking about the relationship between strategic plan and brand strategy has created opportunities for his company to work in partnership with AKA Strategy, a firm that specializes in facilitating strategic plans for nonprofits, including colleges and universities. AKA observes, "While the strategic plan contains the vision and goals required to be effective, it often lacks the emotional storytelling power that helps an institution get its stakeholders excited, engaged, and bought-in to the plan's new directions. Enhanced ability to look at strategy and storyline together" is the basis of these firms' partnership:

> Our clients have found that our combined efforts result in clearer and more compelling strategic plans—plans that get stakeholders excited about the institution and inspired to do more for it—to give it their attention, time, financial and vocal support. . . . Our clients are increasingly asking our help in translating the vision and strategies we create with them into a distinctive brand and a communications strategy to make it resonate with diverse stakeholder groups. Put simply, when an organization thinks about both its strategy and how to tell its story at the same time, it works more efficiently and improves the quality of both its vision and the messages it uses to convey that vision.[17]

Of course, one can't always determine the order in which things are done. An institution with a strategic plan already in place that is in need of brand development or refinement should use the former to help shape the latter. Bill Faust, a partner at Ologie, a branding and marketing agency who has helped many colleges and universities develop and express their brand strategy, advises, "Ideally, there is an institutional strategy that informs brand strategy. If I think about those two things as circles, where they overlap in a Venn diagram is the area of mission, vision, and values. Of all the things that come out of an institutional strategy, those have the most currency for a brand strategy. If an institution hasn't thought those through, that makes it makes it hard for the branding work."[18]

Indeed. Once, I was called to consult with a private university in the Northeast that was trying to think about how to help its marketing team prepare for a branding effort. Asked where to begin, I suggested that they start with elements of the strategic plan. They looked at one another and then shared, somewhat sheepishly, that they had no such plan and that they had been operating without one for years under a president who had been in place for decades. Their direction as an institution was at best unclear and at worst adrift, and they had no existing foundation to which they could anchor their brand. They needed a strategic direction and a closely aligned brand strategy, and eventually, under new leadership, they got both.

In summary, a process of brand strategy development that is designed to build value in relation to an institution's highest-priority strategic goals, will be informed by and/or closely linked to the development of its strategic plan. If an institution's strategic planning is outdated, it makes sense to undertake these processes together, starting with market research that informs both. If the plan is in place and still vital, then it should strongly inform and serve as one foundational element of any development or refinement of brand strategy.

Using Marketing Strategy to Meet Strategic Goals

The experience, background, and interests of presidents, provosts, board members, and those responsible for leading higher education marketing efforts can be quite varied, which can strongly influence expectations about the purpose of marketing and the relationship to overall strategy. In addition, the experience of leaders, the strategic goals that marketing should address, and the institutional context (size, position in the market) play an important role in determining what investment and organizational capacity is necessary to successfully implement marketing plans.

This book is designed to help higher education leaders learn to confidently structure, resource, and evaluate strategic marketing efforts. Chapters 1–5 define and introduce leaders to the strategic value of marketing, establish its foundation in market research, and describe how to deploy it in service of strategic goals. Chapter 6 provides an overview of the practice and tools of digital marketing—just enough to provide sufficient consumer knowledge—so that leaders can ask informed questions, establish clear goals, evaluate the institutional capacity, and identify the best leaders and partners. Chapter 7 covers the landscape of marketing measurement so that leaders can hold CMOs accountable for effective efforts. In chapters 8 and 9, discussions of investment and future trends provide leaders with the knowledge they need to successfully employ strategic integrated marketing practices now and anticipate how they might evolve in one of the most challenging periods in higher education's history. At the end of each chapter, as here, key questions are offered to prompt productive discussions between institutional leaders and their CMOs about how to use the power of strategic marketing to build revenue and reputation for the benefit and health of their institutions.

Key Questions for Leaders and Their CMOs

- How do we view the purpose of marketing?

- How does our strategic planning intersect with our brand strategy?

Chapter 1

The Basics

_ _

What Is Marketing, and How Do We Do
It in Higher Education?

Institutions have focused almost exclusively on the promotional
aspect of marketing, and it is this limited definition that is usually at
the root of both their distrust of the process and their underestimation of its potential benefits.

—Bob Sevier, senior vice-president, Stamats

To appreciate the strategic nature of integrated marketing
and its central purpose to build value—revenue, support, and
reputation—a comprehensive definition is needed to broaden
understanding, dispel common myths, and demonstrate that marketing is well suited in the context of nonprofit higher education.
Understanding the definition and purpose of marketing is a crucial
foundation for its most effective and impactful use.

A Proper Definition in the Context of Higher Education

Academic bias toward marketing is rooted in a misunderstand-
ing of what *marketing* really means. Until recently, terms such
as *markets* and *marketing* had little currency in higher education.
A marketing text for college admissions officers published in the
early 1980s warned that these terms "often grate on academic

ears—particularly those that are attached to heads that fail to comprehend that marketing is not a synonym for advertising."[1]

In the earliest years of marketing practice in higher education, institutions focused primarily on only one dimension: promotion. Robert Sevier explains the challenges of this limited view: "Institutions have focused almost exclusively on the promotional aspect of marketing, and it is this limited definition that is usually at the root of both their distrust of the process and their underestimation of its potential benefits. In the minds of administrators, staff, and faculty, a promotion-only definition of marketing leads only to gimmickry and hyperbole. Marketing at this level is often distilled to the notion of buying a bigger billboard or creating slick publications."[2]

A more complete and proper definition for *marketing*, especially in the context of a nonprofit institution providing educational services and programs, was first established by Philip Kotler at Northwestern's Kellogg School of Management: "the analysis, planning, implementation, and control of carefully formulated programs designed to bring about voluntary and satisfying exchanges of values with target markets for the purpose of achieving organizational objectives."[3] In my experiences with university stakeholders, this definition successfully translates a business process to an educational context, since it aligns beautifully with the values of nonprofit institutions. At the root of the definition is the notion of exchange of values between two parties. Students and families pay tuition dollars to colleges in return for education, credentials, experiences, and preparation for—or enhancement of—careers. Alumni provide time as volunteers and advocates in exchange for meaningful experiences and connections with networks of other alumni. Donors make philanthropic gifts in exchange for recognition or a sense of altruism or to have an impact in areas of knowledge or parts of the institution they care about most deeply.

Such exchanges must meet two criteria: they must be voluntary and satisfying. There's no room for trickery, spinning, or misrepresentation. A student willingly pays tuition based on an authentic offer or promise made during the recruitment and admission process, one that must be delivered in order to be satisfying. To be satisfying, what is offered must be delivered, and the exchange must be equitable or reciprocated. If the promise has been misrepresented, if the institution fails to deliver, or if the exchange disproportionately serves the interests of the institution over the student's (i.e., if it's a "rip-off"), it is not likely to be repeated, and the institution's reputation suffers in the market as a result. Within this framework, student attrition represents a failed marketing exchange, while retention represents a successful one. A gift from a faithful annual donor represents a successful exchange, as does the action of a lifetime member of the alumni association and the alumna who regularly attends reunions, homecoming, or other signature campus events.

Kotler's definition also puts the development of these exchanges in a strategic context that is rooted in research and planning and is connected directly to the achievement of high-level institutional goals. "Successful marketing efforts are based on a careful, research-based appraisal of an institution's internal and external environment," writes Sevier.[4] The exchanges relate directly to the outcomes and priorities targeted in the institution's strategic plan, including enrollment, retention, student satisfaction, fundraising, recognition, and reputation.

Moreover, Kotler emphasizes the discipline of marketing when he refers to "implementation" and "control" of "carefully formulated programs." This is a reference to the marketing mix known as the "Four Ps"—a combination of price, product, place, and promotion.[5] This mix emphasizes that shaping and implementing a strategic marketing plan involves consideration of the price at which programs and services are offered; the distinguishing features and benefits of these programs and services; the means by which they are accessed (when, where, and how, e.g., in a specific place or via technology); and the strategy, messages, and means used to promote them.

Lastly, Kotler refers to "target markets" in the exchange between an institution and those it hopes to engage. A market, write Larry Litten, Daniel Sullivan, and David Brodigan, is "an aggregation of individuals or organizations that seek to obtain certain benefits or satisfy certain needs or desires through the products provided by others."[6] Target markets can be divided into market segments. A market segment is a group of people who share characteristics, behaviors, desires, needs, perceptions, or other phenomena that differ from those of other groups within the market. Segments are commonly defined by objective attributes (race, age, gender, geography, occupation, education, religion) and subjective ones (values and perceptions).[7]

The "demand" side of the equation in the exchange represents the people or organizations whose needs are met—customers or consumers—while suppliers or providers satisfy the demand.[8] The customers in higher education exchanges most often provide money, time, support, advocacy, or some combination of those in exchange for institutional providers' programs, services, networks, recognition, sense of altruism, or associations with the institution's quality and reputation. Extending the exchange framework further, public officials provide financial support in return for educated citizens, satisfied businesses and employers, and extensions of applied research and service to the citizens of their state, region, or nation. Even foundations and funding agencies enter an exchange, providing research and contract funds in return for scholarship and service that addresses critical problems or furthers knowledge and understanding in areas associated with their missions.

Describing and illustrating marketing as an exchange puts a university's strategic goals in a context of satisfying needs to build institutional value. For academic audiences, in particular, this translation of marketing from a strictly business context to one that uses terms and examples familiar in the Academy generates greater comfort with and acceptance of the term.

Market, customer, and *supplier* are technical terms that developed around product marketing in a business context, and nothing raises the hackles of faculty and some academic leaders more than expressions implying that higher education is a business, education is a product, and students are customers whose needs define what should be taught despite their lack of experience or sophistication with pedagogy, curriculum, and traditions of academic disciplines. Rather than creating an obstacle that hinders an appreciation of the strategic value of marketing, a translation of these terms to a context more appropriate in our academic culture is recommended. What technical precision is lost in the translation is balanced by the gains of understanding and openness to learning about and embracing an approach that is intended to improve success on key institutional outcomes, about which campus communities care deeply.

Markets, for example, may be referred to as *audiences,* representing key segments of people whose characteristics and needs or desires are shared. Customers or consumers within these markets can be referred to as *constituents* or *stakeholders* or by the broadest names for their segments—*students, alumni, donors, community members, legislators,* and so on. Suppliers can be called *providers* when a term other than *college, university,* or *department* is necessary. Other providers seeking to enter exchanges of value with the same audiences for similar programs and services are *competitors.* Successful institutions beat their competitors by differentiating their *brand* and *value proposition*—terms defined in the pages ahead—from others.

The notion of suppliers or providers leads to an important conversation about product versus services marketing, one that addresses the objections of treating students as customers, education as a commodity, and faculty and staff as suppliers. Without diminishing the noble work of faculty and staff, whose expertise plays a critical role in deciding what programs will be offered, we may refer to higher education marketing as a form of services marketing. After all, education is a service industry, and "although the 'core business' of an institution of higher learning is, of course, education, colleges and universities are actually simultaneously in several services businesses," including hospitality (residence halls and dining services), entertainment (athletic and other programs that offer concerts, lectures, movies, and museum exhibits), financial services (financial aid and student accounts), and health services (health and counseling centers), all in addition to the business of providing education.[9] Moreover, higher education institutions measure satisfaction with the experience, as service industries do, through student satisfaction and campus climate surveys because we know that satisfaction is an important factor in retaining our stakeholders in exchanges of value.

The Marketing Mix

Viewing Kotler's definition of nonprofit marketing in the context of services marketing, where *product* can signify educational programs and services, gives us a useful definition of higher education marketing. Success in meeting strategic goals depends upon insights gleaned from research about an institution, its competitors, and its markets. These insights inform key institutional decisions, which affect stakeholder choices to enter exchanges of value. Using the framework of the marketing mix, decisions about price, product, place, and promotion all play a role. Price decisions include rate setting for annual tuition, fees, room and board, and expenses, as well as net price (after tuition discounting or institutional financial aid). Product decisions represent all the choices about the academic programs and services the institution offers. Place decisions represent choices about access to the programs and services, ranging from on-campus course offerings (frequency and times of sections), to the business hours during which departments and services offices are open, to the number of starts per year for online programs and the access to courseware that provides the place for online learning to occur. Promotion decisions refer to the message strategy and channels that will be used to reach segments of the target markets.

Any one of the factors in the marketing mix can distinguish an institution from its competitors, and taken together, they represent the offer the institution makes in the exchange of value. Thus, truly integrated, strategic marketing involves leaders including the president, the provost, and the chief financial officer and key faculty and staff leaders, among others, not just the CMO, and success in creating satisfying marketing exchanges is about a lot more than developing a tagline, logo, or key messages that will be used as themes throughout an academic year.

Value Proposition and Positioning

A *value proposition* is basically a program, service, innovation, or feature on which an organization focuses to attract customers.[10] It is a communicated promise of value, designed to facilitate an exchange, and one that must be delivered. Any or all of the elements of the marketing mix can be used to develop a differentiated value proposition in a market. An internal marketing tool that is used to provide message discipline in service of the value proposition is a *positioning statement*, which explains what benefit an institution provides, for whom, and how the institution does it distinctively well. It describes the organization's target audience or constituent, the problem it solves, and why it is distinctly better than the alternatives provided by competitors. The terms *value proposition* and *positioning statement* are not used in marketing materials; rather they guide institutional strategy and decisions that will facilitate exchanges with target audiences and build value.

Colleges and universities are notorious for choosing and expressing value propositions that are decidedly undifferentiated and all things to all audiences. Like many institutional strategic plans, positioning statements that try to serve all interests and do not make choices are not at all strategic. Academic leaders and faculty must resist their inclination to describe how they are similar to other (usually aspirational competitor) institutions, often in lengthy and precise academic prose, and instead briefly, courageously, and clearly state how they are different. Such focused choices will result in some audiences not choosing an institution, but being clear and compelling encourages people in target audiences to identify and choose a satisfying exchange of value.

It is worth noting that differentiating on mission alone is tough. With more than 3,300 nonprofit institutions in the United States alone,[11] all essentially offering education and human development to prepare graduates for productive and meaningful lives and to advance society, choosing to stick to the four corners of the mission statement is not going to help target audiences choose one institution over its competitors.

The challenges of developing a differentiated value proposition are illustrated in the following positioning statements of three different types of institutions. Each takes a slightly different form, but they share a structure that includes a narrative to describe the positioning and a series of claims that are intended to declare the institution's distinctive value. They are based on actual statements but have been edited for length and to remove identifying information.

Small Liberal Arts College Positioning Statement
Midwest College is located at the intersection of academics and opportunity. Our commitment to the liberal arts, faith, and service, and our city location means that education extends far beyond the classroom, with unmatched undergraduate research, internship, service, entrepreneurial, and global experiences for our students. We're a vibrant and diverse campus community made up of more than 3,000 students from 30 states and 25 countries. On our beautiful green campus, students form life-long friendships, make lasting memories and explore their faith.

Small Liberal Arts College Value Proposition

- an unpretentious community where students, professors, and staff care deeply about each other
- professors who collaborate with students to enhance learning
- a global perspective through extensive international experiences
- undergraduate research opportunities and a rigorous and challenging academic experience
- performing and visual arts as central to a well-rounded liberal arts education.
- involvement in intercollegiate athletics
- vast resources of the local region provide internships, clinical practice, student teaching, part- and full-time employment
- students graduate in four years, unlike at public universities in the region
- preparation for careers through hands-on learning
- measurable outcomes

To its credit, this college differentiates its position among competitors in the market based on its faith-based mission, its location, and its community. And among its value proposition claims, it differentiates itself from large public institutions that don't graduate students in four years at the same rates and from institutions located in more rural regions that don't have the same resources and opportunities. However, those distinctive factors would be less compelling if the competitors for target audiences included other liberal arts colleges or other institutions in thriving cities. Moreover, the length of these statements (which were lightly edited here for length) has the net effect of burying the most differentiating factors with a basket of items that most institutions claim, many of them table stakes that an institution of higher education should be expected to deliver. The difficulty in getting an institution to make choices about the primary reasons that students (or other audiences) choose it is reflected in the length and comprehensiveness of these statements. Unfortunately, any attempt to express all the ideas will result in strategies and messages that are diffuse and undifferentiated.

Large Research University Positioning Statement
We offer students an extraordinary and diverse educational experience that inspires creativity, self-discovery, and leadership, which will benefit them for a lifetime. Alumni enjoy lifelong pride, distinction, and a global network of invaluable connections. Faculty and staff find opportunities that amplify creative expression and inspire discovery, professional integrity, distinction, and advancement. We foster the health and vitality of our local community through education, service, research, and the arts. With our business partners, we enhance economic opportunity, diversity, innovation, and effectiveness, and we champion and practice environmental sustainability, conservation, and the highest levels of efficiency.

Large Research University Value Proposition
- creativity fostered through culture and character
- community that enhances our sense of place
- competitiveness, not for rivalry but to improve, innovate, and succeed
- engagement in a student-centered environment
- opportunity to advance or progress
- preeminence to uphold the public's trust in our quality and innovation in research, teaching, and service
- resourcefulness and efficiency to steward public funds in challenging fiscal circumstances
- respect and high standards for academics, sportsmanship, positive attitudes, and helping others

This large, public research university aims to distinguish itself from competitors based on creativity and discovery, which might give it an edge in relation to public institutions in the region, ones that are not so research intensive. It also attempts to integrate the importance of intercollegiate athletics and research as core elements of the institution under the banner of competitiveness. However, the positioning statement does not facilitate differentiation from other large research universities with strong athletic programs with which it likely competes, and like the college whose statement preceded it, it tries to be all things to all people.

Having guided the development of positioning language through the process of socialization, input, and adoption at two universities, I'm sympathetic. Communities within institutions want to see themselves and their part of the institution in these statements, and compromise is often necessary to arrive at consensus support. However, leaders who champion differentiation in the early stages of positioning or repositioning their institutions, and who articulate its critical role in inspiring exchanges that build value, are likely to be more successful in arriving at a strategic position that constituents will recognize and choose over similar positions. (How to arrive at a distinctive position is discussed further in chapter 4.)

One other observation about the value proposition at the large university is worth noting. Instead of expressing the distinctive value of the institution in terms of how it meets a recognized need of the target audience, the university gravitates to an institutional expression of its values. Arriving at common values is a lot easier. Institutions' history, mission, and vision statements are laden with values that in many cases have guided them for years. While both value proposition and values are important, they are not the same, and they don't serve the same purpose. Values are expressed to guide communities and are most relevant internally, while value propositions recognize the specific needs or desires that the institution meets in some distinctive way (relevant to target audiences, critical if it will serve as the basis for motivating an engaging exchange of value). Marketing communication is a two-way process, one that focuses more on listening, learning, and recognizing the value for the audience in the exchange than most institutions are inclined to do.

In an effort to provide an exemplary alternative, consider this "strategic vision" offered by a university in the leadership profile used to search for its next president:

Medium-Sized Public Regional Comprehensive University Positioning
The University is an access-driven, urban-serving comprehensive university that provides a world-class education and promotes economic growth and sustainability as well as health, wellness, and social equity in our city and the surrounding areas through a commitment to interdisciplinary learning, scholarship, and problem-solving.

We're on a mission . . . to create a university reflective of the needs and potential of the state's third largest city, one that plays an essential and expanded role in making our residents happier, healthier, and better prepared for the future.

While the language in this statement is oriented more toward higher education leaders and academics than toward students, its laser focus on place-based needs of its region and its impact on the community are simple and relevant. To the extent that this university occupies a distinctive position relative to its competitors, this may be a very powerful source of regional differentiation.

These examples demonstrate the challenge of choosing an institutional position that both distinguishes the institution from its competitors and is relevant to primary audiences. There's a third criteria for an effective positioning, and it should be obvious: it should be true. Authenticity is a must for internal audiences and for those whom an institution hopes to engage. Moreover, that authenticity must be based in accurate self-awareness. An institution with high admit rates and low ratings by students on the National Survey of Student Engagement (NSSE) related to academic challenge and the amount of time spent studying cannot credibly claim a proposition of academic rigor, for example. If there is too much aspiration and not enough reality, internal constituents will not buy in, and external audiences will fail to believe. An early marketing mentor taught me long ago that an effective position is both a mirror and a bridge. It should reflect who you are, as well as where you are going. If there is too much bridge and not enough mirror, the position will be sniffed out as inauthentic and won't serve as the basis for a satisfying exchange of value.

Taken together, authenticity, differentiation, and relevance should be the guideposts for strong institutional positioning statements that express the value proposition for target audiences, what a government-funded project in the United Kingdom, the Distinct project, called the three Rs—real, rare, and relevant.[12]

A good exercise for any leader is to review their institution's positioning statement, if it has one, or to test a developing position. First, omit any reference to the name of the institution. Could the statement describe many institutions, especially within one's competitive market? If so, it is not rare and not doing its job. Second, does it specifically address recognized needs or desires of the primary audiences or stakeholders, whose engagement and support are crucial to building value? Or does it describe the institution from the perspective of internal constituencies? If the latter statement is true, it may not be relevant. Third, is it mostly a reflection of the current institution, with a bit of aspiration sprinkled in? If so, it is real.

In short, making choices about institutional positioning is challenging but necessary if the positioning is to be effective. Authenticity (real), differentiation (rare), and recognition of the value that audiences seek (relevant) are all important elements of positioning.

Brand, Brand Marketing, and Brand Strategy

The first building blocks of strategic integrated marketing are a value proposition and a positioning statement, but they are not the only elements of a strong brand strategy, which organizes institutional decisions and communication to reinforce a small number of ideas that deliver on the promise in the exchanges of value. This process is discussed in greater detailed in chapter 4. For purposes of setting the baseline, *brand* and *branding* are defined here.

The "B-word" is another one of those terms that turn academics off very quickly, given its association with consumer products and commercial business. "Trying to sell a university as if it were a box of Cocoa Puffs was thought to be financially suspect, not to mention unseemly," Andrea Naddaff, vice-president for business at Corey McPherson Nash (a marketing agency) told the *Chronicle of Higher Education* in 2003.[13] Naddaff recalled a time when "educators would take umbrage" at the suggestion that their institutions could benefit from marketing, but that was no longer the case. They started calling her. "Branding is not a dirty word anymore," she said.

One of my favorite gadflies on the faculty at the University of Maryland was quoted by the *Chronicle* in the same article: "I'm very skeptical of these marketing efforts and their value. It's not like we are selling toothpaste." And yet, faculty are often quick to complain, "We don't do a good enough job of telling our story."

Suffice to say that though marketing has come of age in higher education, there's still work to do, especially to bring faculty along. This is another occasion to translate the word *brand* and explain the advantages of such a tool in the context of academic culture and strategic institutional goals. There are literally dozens of definitions of *brand* in marketing literature, but some of the best include those of Kotler and Karen Fox and of Kevin Keller.[14] Some common and important themes from this literature about brand include:

- A brand exists in the minds of your audiences, not yours.
- A brand is the sum total of experiences and associations that a customer has with your organization. Everything you say and do in your interactions with audiences shapes their sense of your brand.

- Every institution has a brand; it is only a question of whether it is being well managed or not.

Strong and effective brands provide advantages. They motivate people to engage in exchanges of value over and above any messaging about a particular program or service.[15] Strong brands motivate people to exchange value, even at a higher price. Institutions with weak brands experience price elasticity; their ability to engage audiences in an exchange of value is very sensitive to changes in price. On the other hand, strong brands are relatively inelastic; price increases do not substantially diminish their demand (think Harvard or Stanford). Strong brands protect institutions in a crisis. Audiences who are strong supporters—who demonstrate brand loyalty through repeated engagement—are more likely to see a negative event as an exception to the rule in regard to the institution they admire or love, while stakeholders of an institution with a weak brand are likely to consider a negative event as indicative of everything that is wrong with it. So strong brands build value in terms of revenue and reputation.

Branding, or the use of brand marketing to influence the perception of a brand in the minds of an institution's audience to motivate exchanges of value, is a framework for developing and measuring an institution's relationships with members of target audiences (fig. 1).[16]

Keller's brand equity model comprises four steps that an organization must follow to develop and deepen its relationship with customers. The steps relate to questions that customers ask and the organization must answer effectively in order to engage in an exchange of value and sustain a satisfying relationship.

First, an institution must establish brand awareness or salience to develop recognition by standing out and effectively registering its identity. Next, an institution establishes brand meaning through performance and imagery. The institution begins to build equity by developing an understanding of who it is, what it

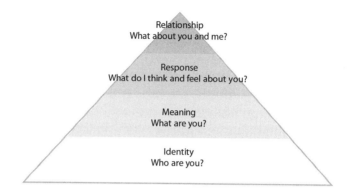

Relationship
What about you and me?

Response
What do I think and feel about you?

Meaning
What are you?

Identity
Who are you?

Figure 1. Keller's brand equity model, reflecting stages of development in relationships with customers. Adapted from Kevin Lane Keller, *Strategic Brand Management* (Upper Saddle River, NJ: Prentice-Hall, 1998).

stands for, and how well offerings match a customer's needs and expectations. An institution creates greater likelihood of engagement and support by establishing strong, positive, and differentiating associations with its brand through experiences, advertising, and word of mouth, for example. Then, customers respond by making judgments about an institution's quality, credibility, fit, and superiority relative to competitors and by establishing feelings about the institution or about themselves in relation to the brand. Positive feelings and judgments lead to initial brand support or engagement. And finally, at the apex of deep and sustainable relationships with the institution, customers repeatedly engage and support the brand, recommend it to others, feel a sense of attachment, and connect with and identify with a community of other customers.

On a continuum from weak to strong relationships, institutions seek to move target audiences from no awareness and weak relationships to supportive relationships based on engagement in a desired exchange of value. The deepest and most desirable relationships between an individual and the institution are reflected in repeated engagement and brand loyalty.

A *brand strategy* is a tool for organizing an institution's integrated marketing and communication, as well as its offerings and experiences, to establish exchanges of value with audiences and to deepen and sustain these relationships to build value in the form of revenue, reputation, and brand equity. Recall that the Four Ps include not just promotion but price, product, and place as well. If brand marketing promises something that the institution does not deliver, no messaging will solve that problem.

Development of a brand strategy is based on insight about customers or stakeholders and their perceptions of an institution and its competitors. Ideally, the brand strategy is closely aligned and integrated with the priorities in an institution's strategic plan, since the plan reflects investments in the programs, services, and experiences for which audiences are exchanging value. A brand strategy reflects a positioning statement, which expresses the distinctive value position, but also considers or expresses an institution's image, reputation, personality, culture, and values. (More on that in chapter 4.) Since it incorporates the value proposition, by definition a brand strategy must be real (authentic), rare (differentiating), and relevant (meaningful to target audiences). To this, one more criterion for an effective brand strategy must be added: it must be simple and memorable.

Examine the earlier examples of positioning in this chapter or review your institution's current or developing one. How long is it, and how many items does it include? If someone unfamiliar with the institution read it, how much would they recall afterward? Audiences do not retain multiple attributes or associations about institutions in their minds, even about institutions to which they express loyalty; more than three or four would be impractical. If it takes a lot of ideas and words to express the brand, it won't serve as the foundation or discipline for clear, recognizable, and compelling communication to audiences about the institution. A brand strategy should be organized around a small number of priorities for communication, investment, and reinforcement in every interaction with audiences.

Now that the terms have been defined, translated to a context that aligns with academic culture, and illustrated in ways that reflect the strategic nature of integrated marketing to build value for institutions, we turn to how organizations lead, organize, and structure their marketing efforts.

Key Questions for Leaders and Their CMOs

- What differentiates us? What is our positioning strategy in the market?

- What is our current level of brand awareness in the market? What are we known for? Are we trying to change what we're known for or reinforce and strengthen the current perception?

- What role should our CMO play in conversations related to programs and pricing strategy?

Chapter 2

Getting Started or Starting Fresh

Leadership, Assessment, and Organizational Structure

Organizational structure is the biggest barrier to integrated
marketing and branding on college campuses.
                —Elizabeth Johnson, chairman, SimpsonScarborough

Building marketing capacity within the institution is not undertaken lightly and usually doesn't begin with a decision to hire a
chief marketing officer or to develop a marketing and communication division out of whole cloth. For decades, institutions have
hired professionals with marketing experience in discrete areas,
like admissions, the annual fund, development, or university relations. But in terms of higher education history, the concept of
an institution-wide marketing function led by a senior manager
or executive is a relatively recent phenomenon. In the early
1980s, when marketing was just beginning to take root in admissions offices, few could fathom the idea of a vice-president of
marketing leading a marketing function. Some said it was highly
unlikely that it would ever occur, though Philip Kotler, the nonprofit marketing visionary, had suggested it.[1] Even a decade ago,
very few colleges and universities began their foray into strategic
integrated marketing by hiring an executive-level vice-president
of marketing. Rather, an institution with no such capacity was

more likely to begin with a mid-level director of marketing in a one-person shop, serving as a resource or internal consultant to other offices or divisions.[2]

My own entry to the field was a similar, if short-lived, setup. In the mid-1990s, the president and the vice-president for university relations at my alma mater contemplated how best to start. The president had recently received counsel from a member of the public university system's board of regents, who was the head of a major advertising agency with powerhouse corporate clients. The regent had observed that the University of Maryland would never realize its aspirations for greater distinction and reputation if it did not get the many strong and independent parts of the institution to work together in more integrated manner on a shared message strategy. So the leadership posted a position description for a full-time marketing director who would report to the vice-president for university advancement and serve as a peer to the director of media relations and the director of publications. Having served as the first marketing manager in undergraduate admissions, I was encouraged to apply. After I reviewed the job description (which had interpreted the role as primarily to "coordinate the messages of the deans") and learned more about the early setup (no administrative assistant, no staff, budget to be determined), I thanked the leadership but decided not to apply. When pressed, I told the search committee that I didn't think the position was set up to succeed.

That led to an invitation to speak with leaders about what success would look like. I shared an earnest description of the strategic marketing effort that was needed, including identification of target audiences, research that reflected their perceptions and a more foundational need to arrive at a strategy to differentiate from competitors and increase recognition and support for the institution's special mission and quality as the flagship research university of the state. I was met with modest interest and amusement at my moxie.

Clearly, the leadership had something more tactical in mind: an internal consultant or advisor equipped with an operating budget of $48,000 to get those deans working together! I told them I would not continue in the search, but I offered to help find someone else. After a short period of consideration, they proposed an alternative: I could continue as a candidate, and if I was selected, they would consider my input on how to set it up for success. In the end, we agreed to the latter.

In 1997 I was appointed as the University of Maryland's first marketing director, with an administrative assistant and a first-year budget double the first offer. Within six months (and I suspect after another conversation with that wise and experienced regent), a new vice-president for university advancement appointed me to lead the three units in advancement communication (marketing, media relations, and university publications). With the input of the vice-president and the leaders of these units, I began to restructure the human and financial resources for a more comprehensive and strategic approach to marketing the institution.

Some institutions put a toe in the water by first seeking outside, ad hoc help from marketing consulting firms, research firms, advertising agencies, or public relations firms. Such efforts may begin to produce elements or foundations of a marketing program. These resources are most effective when the consultants are asked to address a specific marketing task or project, such as the design of a visual identity (logo) system; production of print or digital materials for a campaign for undergraduate admissions; or development of a theme and collateral for the launch of a fundraising campaign. Discrete projects like these produce excellent value in the short term. However, they don't accomplish what a marketing-oriented organization that provides strategic integrated marketing as a framework for building value can accomplish. Eventually, an institution that is serious about establishing a marketing mind-set must bring the marketing function in-house and make it a formal department or division.[3]

Leaders want to understand how to structure their marketing organization for success, how to choose marketing leadership, and how to build a team or hire partners that will help to set priorities, gain support, and account for results. Whether an institution is starting from scratch and wants to build a strategic marketing function or is looking to develop that capacity with an existing team, this chapter reviews important considerations for leadership; reporting; common organizational structures by both size and type of institution; consideration of roles and responsibilities at both university and unit levels and how to integrate them through structure and process; and strategies for assessing organizational capacity in relation to priorities.

Who Leads the Effort?

Institutions can take very different approaches to leading and staffing a strategic communication and marketing function. It is difficult to separate the decision about who should lead from the decision about what they should lead—what structure and capacities will be needed in the context of the institution's needs. Here, we'll tackle the leadership decision first and follow with the choices of structure and capacity, mindful that the two are necessarily intertwined.

Often, the leader reflects the skills and experiences that the president and board think are necessary to meet strategic goals. While there is no standard organizational structure from which we might draw, there are some common themes. Institutions more driven by enrollment and those trying to reposition themselves or dramatically change their position in the marketplace were more likely to be early adopters of a strategic integrated marketing framework to organize their capacity, and they therefore sought leaders with a marketing background. Those maintaining or protecting an existing reputation and strong brand, as well as those who are not as sensitive to a changing enrollment demand, may be more likely to choose public relations or public affairs professionals to lead their efforts. This is especially true if important goals and priorities are related to influencing elected officials through advocacy, garnering support for federal research funding, or engaging opinion leaders outside the higher education sector.

The communication and marketing leader should have demonstrated experience related to the approach and preferences of the president as well as to the goals to be achieved.[4] Since the vast majority of institutions (80%) integrate their marketing and communication functions in one structure led by one chief,[5] seasoned public relations and media professionals have recognized the need to become adept in the use marketing tools to build value, just as seasoned marketing professionals have understood the value of shaping and aligning media and PR strategies with the overall brand strategy.

Educational Background

Training and expertise in marketing, public relations, and strategic communication are the best qualifications for the chief marketing and communication position, although related fields like journalism, literature, and education can provide a solid foundation. My own degrees in English and education (specifically higher education and college student development) provided excellent foundations, but they did not prepare me to learn marketing theory and practice at the level required to lead. Professionals with degrees in related fields who have availed themselves of significant professional development opportunities through the American Marketing Association (AMA, specifically the Symposium for the Marketing of Higher Education) and CASE can, if they obtain progressively responsible experience, develop the set of competencies that are required to do this work.

It is worth noting that because leadership in higher education often benefits from the credibility of an advanced degree, although an MBA, a master's degree, or a doctorate isn't required, it can be helpful, especially when dealing with faculty in departments of marketing, communication, and journalism on a campus. My own PhD in education has proved invaluable in my relationships with faculty, who know that I have a better understanding of their scholarly responsibilities as a result of my own training and work.

Experience in Higher Education or Other Sectors

CMO experience may come from within or outside the higher education sector, for the profession of marketing in higher education hasn't existed long enough to produce a sufficient supply of marketing leaders who are native to higher education. Though the field of higher education marketing is coming of age, its relative immaturity compared with other administrative functions means that there haven't been enough marketing professionals with training and experience in the sector.

That's changing, with the growth of professional development training in organizations like CASE and the American Marketing Association, which hosts the largest annual gathering of higher education marketing professionals in the world. Attendance at the AMA's thirtieth-anniversary Symposium for the Marketing of Higher Education in 2019 numbered 1,400 participants, an increase of 250 percent over the last two decades, far exceeding attendance at AMA meetings for marketers in any other sector. As the field matures and professionals who started in the higher education sector rise to the ranks of leadership, there will be more leaders with native (i.e., innate and instinctive) expertise.

Meanwhile, institutional leaders have often relied on talent borrowed from the corporate, nonprofit, and government sectors.[6] These CMOs bring skills and expertise, but they may not understand academic culture or have an appreciation for the time and effort it takes to develop support in a shared governance environment. They may underestimate how important it is to slow down and consult broadly, gathering input and building buy-in for initiatives that represent the identity of the institution and that aim to influence its reputation among many constituencies. Kim Whitler, a former CMO and senior contributor at Forbes, underlines the value of hiring those who can bring needed skills and respect the culture. "Leaders with an ability to navigate bureaucracy can chart a new course and make a real difference."[7]

I have met higher education leaders who believe that academic marketers aren't tough enough to deal with the myriad internal stakeholders and units with powerful sub-brands within their own organizations (e.g., named medical, business, and law schools, well-known research centers). They believe a CMO needs toughness and experience outside the sector to break through the resistance and silos that often characterize the lack of willingness of independent or semiautonomous schools and departments to participate in marketing at an enterprise level. Whether the CMO's experience is in higher education or in the corporate, government, or nonprofit sector, he or she must demonstrate an ability to read and respect the academic culture and to respect long-standing values and traditions, especially shared governance and the need to develop consensus around key institutional decisions and initiatives.

Those coming from corporate or government settings often mistakenly expect the pace of the university setting to be slower, more relaxed, and less demanding, but of course nothing could be further from the truth. They may be unfamiliar with the broad higher education landscape, with strong headwinds buffeting the sector, including demographic trends, increased levels of accountability, declining public support, and questions about the value of a college degree. Moreover, understanding university relationships and politics is a daunting task for which many outside higher education are unprepared. The "pace of decision making and the presence of lateral decision processes may be entirely foreign to many individuals who come from industry," writes Thomas Hayes. Further, those whose experience is from marketing of consumer goods may know very little about marketing a service, which, we have established, higher education marketing includes. For this reason, Hayes recommends considering candidates from service industries and nonprofits.[8]

Indeed, when I visited the chief experience officer and the patient experience team at the Cleveland Clinic, one of the most renowned hospitals in the world, I found that health care marketers in particular work in a similarly competitive marketplace and understand the need to respond to rapidly changing demographics and expectations for customer service. Moreover, the parallels between hospital and university staff and between physicians and faculty are remarkable, so CMOs from the healthcare sector will have the advantage of being familiar with very powerful internal stakeholders and the dynamics between them.

Demonstrated Ability to Act Strategically

Even more important than educational background or professional experience in higher education or other sectors, however, is the ability to think and act strategically. In order to develop a brand strategy or a marketing plan that will help the institution meet its strategic goals and build value, the CMO must be able to develop and cultivate support for smart and well-defined approaches that translate to impact—on revenue, recognition, and reputation. Someone who writes stories about student and faculty successes or creates clever copy for a slogan or email campaign operates primarily in a tactical realm. Such work must be guided by an overarching strategy. What must an institution do to develop awareness among prospects and influencers for the key elements of a major new repositioning strategy? How will the university identify and convert more students for whom the university is their first choice, resulting in higher admissions yield and greater first-year retention? What should the communication plan look like for a fundraising campaign that will place the highest priority on increasing the number of principal gifts from a very small number of high-level prospects with rated capacity to give? Just as leaders choose chief financial officers to build strategies for monetizing assets and growing investments, they need in the chief marketing leader a strategic thinker to build brand equity and shape perceptions that will motivate exchanges of value and stimulate behaviors that support the institution in meeting critical priorities.

Does Reporting Relationship and Title Matter?

The reporting relationship and title influence the marketing leader's success. Increasingly the CMO is part of the executive team. CASE reported that in 2015, 51 percent of the seniormost communication and marketing officers reported to the president or CEO.[9] The higher education CMO surveys in 2014 and 2019 affirmed that half report directly to the president, and in 2019, 56 percent reported that they were members of the president's cabinet or executive leadership team.[10] Since strategic integrated marketing includes not just promotion, but considerations of program, price, and delivery systems, the strategy will intersect with the work of several other members of the executive team.

This shift in reporting is revolutionizing advancement operations at institutions all over the world. Communication was once tucked into the domain of college or university relations, which also included development and alumni relations. In many institutions, particularly large research universities and institutions with a strong and well-known reputation, where public relations and public affairs tools are used to maintain a current position, that's often still the case. However, as strategic integrated marketing matures, as leaders recognize that branding is an enterprise-wide function and that marketing directly influences not just alumni engagement and philanthropy but also enrollment, it is increasingly common for the chief advancement officer to supervise development and alumni relations and for the CMO to serve at the executive level and to lead marketing and communication as strategic institutional functions. Another organizational structure that has emerged is one in which the CMO reports to a vice-president for enrollment. This arrangement has some obvious advantages but the same challenge of limiting the scope of marketing primarily to one strategic domain at the expense of others, and its success usually depends on the willingness of colleagues to collaborate on strategic goals and investments. No matter how the functions are led, philanthropy, marketing, and enrollment all advance institutions, and integrated advancement requires collaboration among the leaders to meet all their important strategic goals, including enrollment, development, and positioning.

The title of those who hold the lead marketing role varies, depending on the institutional context and the structure and functions they lead. Only 8 percent of those in the role literally bore the title CMO in 2014. Another 30 percent were titled director or executive director, 25 percent were titled vice-president, and 14 percent were titled associate vice-president.[11] A CASE survey of communication and marketing trends in 2013 showed that the most senior marketing and communication officers at bachelor's- and master's-level institutions and those at mid-sized (10,001–5,000) and very large institutions (> 25,000) were more likely to hold the title vice-president or assistant vice-president than their counterparts at doctoral institutions and small institutions.[12] However, in 2019 a survey of higher education CMOs revealed that the top marketing official at doctoral- and master's-level institutions was more likely to hold the title vice-president than those at baccalaureate institutions, where they were more likely to be directors.[13]

No matter what titles they hold, top marketing officials have "become firmly entrenched in senior campus leadership," with half reporting to the president or CEO and even more serving as members of the cabinet or executive leadership team.[14] As one of the key leaders in planning for the development of relationships between the institution and its constituencies, the CMO is an integral and valued colleague, providing important counsel prior to critical decisions that will avoid or ameliorate negative reactions from important constituencies. They also ensure that public relations and media strategies—even in a crisis—are aligned with the institution's overall brand values and strategy.

In a multisite case study of the role of CMOs at four-year private institutions, Angela Polec established that CMOs serving as members of the cabinet and those reporting directly to the president possessed significant advantages for establishing the influence necessary not only for their own success but also for the success of the leadership team as a whole. Participation as a member of the executive leadership team allowed the CMOs access to and influence on institutional decisions that related directly to marketing efforts and also created opportunities to establish relationships with other leaders, whose own areas of responsibility could benefit from the CMO's expertise and counsel. One president in her study told Polec that it was for this purpose that he expected and supported his CMO at the outset "to become fully integrated and conversant in every aspect of the University." Moreover, strategy conversations among the leadership benefit from the voice of the customer, market information, and consumer data, which CMOs bring to the table. Finally, CMOs who report to their presidents often serve as a trusted counselor and advisor on myriad issues, informed by the wide lens on the institution that the role offers.[15]

Still, institutions whose presidents come from the academic ranks may prefer a more traditional reporting structure in the integrated advancement model, with an assistant vice-president for marketing reporting to a vice-president for advancement along with the heads of development and alumni relations functions.[16] Keep in mind that this structure can have the limiting effect of siloed marketing focused primarily on advancement, making it challenging to influence, affect, or resource marketing for enrollment or to successfully lead institution-wide branding efforts.

The ideal arrangement for maximum effectiveness includes a seat for the CMO at the leadership table and access to and support from the top. Barring these conditions, other models can work, but only if the executive team agrees to collaborate in developing and sustaining institution-wide marketing and communication strategies.

Setting the Marketing Leader Up for Success

When the lead marketing and communication role reflects understanding of the strategic, executive-level function, the president or CEO designates the marketing leader as a champion, the single person responsible for overall marketing planning and leadership. Robert Sevier articulates the importance of how the role is framed, saying, "At the outset, the marketing champion must be empowered with a clear and demonstrated mandate from the president." This sends an important message to the campus community, supports the stature of the marketing effort as a strategic function, and will be especially important when the marketing leader is called upon to mediate conflicts between units at the institution. The president's support is necessary, but not sufficient, for the marketing leader to be effective. The CMO must be able to galvanize and legitimize marketing efforts and provide accountability to the larger campus community.[17]

Sevier identified four characteristics of strong marketing champions: They must have the respect of the campus community; possess both a theoretical and a practical understanding of marketing; have power and clout or access to power and clout; and be able to lead and motivate people. Further, they must be able to both lead and delegate.[18] These marketers must lead through both management and influence, shaping institutional identity and messaging through everything from admissions materials and Twitter feeds to brand management.[19]

Polec helped us further understand the roles and responsibilities of CMOs, as well as the structures, behaviors, and styles that make them most effective.[20] Given the myriad reporting structures and portfolio compositions of CMOs in higher education, the role has the potential to look different at various institutions. One significant variance in the scope of the CMO position is the role the CMO plays in institutional strategy beyond the traditional promotional and image responsibilities that are associated with marketing and communication.

At the executive level, the CMO not only is responsible for leading the formation of marketing plans and coordinating and supplying marketing services for others but also participates in setting the policy and direction of the entire institution.[21] As noted in the previous chapter, decisions about whether to offer a new program or service, at what rate to set tuition discount levels, and how to deliver access to programs and services are part of the marketing mix and should include the input and counsel of the CMO.

My role as vice-president at American University, for example, included working with the CFO and the vice-provost of enrollment to develop a price elasticity study to inform decisions of the leadership on tuition rates, as well as a lead role in redesigning the student experience to provide a more integrated and holistic undergraduate experience that would improve student retention, well-being, and satisfaction. In addition, when it became clear that explicitly and transparently communicating the value and outcomes of an American University education would give us a strategic advantage, I led a cross-functional team that included the director of the career center and key leaders in institutional research and information technology to develop an interactive website that allowed users to view employment, income, and graduate admission outcomes by degree level and program.[22]

Polec defined these chief marketing officers who operate in a broader, strategic capacity at the institutional level, affecting and contributing to decisions that relate to two or more elements of the marketing mix (beyond promotion, to include product, price, or place), as positioning CMOs, while those operating in a capacity limited primarily to promotional aspects of the marketing mix were classified as promotional CMOs. Despite how their formal responsibilities were defined, she found few differences in the realities of the role, the scope of work, and the institutional impact of positioning CMOs and promotional CMOs. Both types of CMOs were effecting change at the institutional level beyond the scope of marketing and communication.[23]

While Polec's study is limited in terms of generalizability to all CMOs because of her method and the limited number of cases at private institutions, she proposes an interesting framework for successful CMOs to lead and effect change.[24] Polec states that CMOs in higher education need a combination of bureaucratic (formal) and network (informal) power to successfully effect change at their institutions, and identifies key contributors to each type of power.[25]

Polec found two drivers of bureaucratic power in her study: a seat at the leadership table and demonstrated support from the president. She also identified four contributors to the CMO's network power: centrality to operations, strong relationships across campus, data and analytics, and the use of transformational leadership.[26] These should be keys for any institution establishing or renewing its marketing leadership.

To summarize, ideally the person chosen to lead an institution's marketing and communication efforts will be a key contributor to the executive leadership team, reporting to and empowered by the president to provide strategic integrated marketing and communication leadership as well as counsel on key institutional decisions. The CMO should be a strategic thinker and transformational leader—capable of developing strong, collegial relationships with other members of the executive team, the institution's academic leaders, faculty, staff, and students—because they will need to lead through influence as much or more than through assigned, formal responsibility. The CMO's demonstrated experience should align well with leadership preferences and the strategic goals to be achieved, and no matter what sector they come from, they should recognize, appreciate, and respect the academic culture in which they will operate.

Building Organizational Capacity

In addition to leadership and reporting structure, presidents wrestle with the question of internal capacity and functions. The organization's size, expertise, and reporting structure for those who perform marketing and communication functions must be evaluated in the context of the work to be done. Presidents want to know whether the existing team members have the skills and influence to develop strategy and cultivate support from various stakeholders; whether they have credibility and enjoy the trust and confidence of the campus community; and whether they can be objective about the institution's strengths and weaknesses. Larger institutions may have the internal resources to build and sustain capacity in-house. Smaller institutions may need to outsource expertise for project-based work, but they will still need to consider what professionals will be needed to sustain work that has been developed with strategic partners for research, brand strategy, creative development, including ongoing stewardship of the content strategy, and analysis and measurement.

Presidents also wrestle with the question whether an institution that distributes marketing functions can deliver integrated results. They must consider whether the work of marketing staff in a central team and those distributed across divisions and academic units—in functions related to recruitment, enrollment, alumni relations, philanthropy, media and public affairs, digital and social engagement, community and government relations, and athletics—can be sufficiently integrated to effectively implement the strategy.

Provosts, vice-presidents, and other academic leaders are important stakeholders in decisions about the scope of the marketing organization. The investment in staff who perform marketing and communication functions as part of their roles in colleges and schools as well as in other departments or divisions may make the total investment in marketing staff large, but diffuse. If there are not clear structures and policies in place, as well as relationships, to encourage integration of the effort and collaboration in investment and goal-setting, the organizational structure will not be optimized for effectiveness. Most provosts and deans I know are loath to consider structural change that includes direct or matrixed reporting structures for their staff and a chief marketing officer.

Typically, the more widely distributed the marketing responsibilities are, the more diffuse the impact of resources invested. Recently, I consulted with the president of a small liberal arts college in the Northeast who was preparing for a major repositioning effort. The marketing and communication functions had historically been centralized under an office of college advancement, then were distributed among three units: enrollment, college advancement, and central marketing. A lack of alignment around strategy designed to impact major college goals, especially enrollment and retention, was apparent across the staff in the three units. There was no agreement on metrics, and none of the units were leveraging investments in their area for similar needs in another. Ultimately, a decision was made to reintegrate the staff under one leader in the office of college advancement.

Whether the personnel are centralized or distributed, if the best course for building capacity is outsourcing, then choosing the right partners is critical. Just as there are considerations for assessing internal staff, leaders have an interest in identifying partners who represent a good fit with the institution. The maturing of higher education marketing has given rise to a host of agencies and consultants whose expertise and experience is specifically in higher education. Although presidents and board members might feel that a big-name public relations firm or ad agency increase the credibility of their resulting work products, it is critical to work with partners who respect and understand academic culture and who have the seasoning and experience to respectfully push the institution to wrestle with tough choices about differentiation and anchor recommendations about strategy in solid data. If a potential partner does not have other higher education clients, leaders should be careful to evaluate their ability to understand the culture before proceeding.

Board members may have an interest in nominating prospective firms or partners; this is a good use of the members' experience and networks as long as there are no conflicts. Board members may have connections through their own businesses, or they may be able to obtain references or referrals. In this regard, leaders are sometimes tempted with offers of pro bono work. It pays to be cautious. Firms always devote their time and attention to paying clients first; only after they have satisfied those clients do they turn to pro bono work. Ultimately, leaders in mature marketing organizations choose partners on the basis of specific requirements, a specific scope of work, and criteria for making a selection.

There is great variation in the structure for higher education marketing and communication, and there is no apparent standard.[27] However, there is at least evidence that among the vast majority of institutions, college or university strategies for marketing and communication are part of the same organizational function, reporting to one leader.[28] Beyond that, it is difficult to say with certainty what functions, activities, and responsibilities should be included, and where. But the structure isn't an end in itself.[29] It is a means to influence and address the strategic priorities to be achieved, the value the institution needs to build, and the preferences of the CEO in organizing or focusing the effort. To the extent possible, the structure should be flexible and agile, reflecting changes in strategic focus, leadership transitions, and changes resulting from innovations in technology that require evolution.

Size

Institutional leaders who want to establish or assess and refine their marketing capacity often start with a simple question: What are the benchmarks at comparable institutions? Unfortunately, the answer isn't so simple. Since organizational structures vary so widely, it is difficult to gather or provide reliable benchmark data on staff size, especially when institutions are asked to report the total FTEs (full-time equivalents) dedicated to each function. I've personally encountered the difficulty for my own institution of gathering and reporting budget and staffing information across a number of departments or divisions that were not supervised by me as the CMO. It took collaboration with the CFO, the human resources director, and the provost, who encouraged the deans and their marketing/communication staff to provide information. With some effort, we were able to identify staff in offices outside the central marketing and communication division who had some responsibility for marketing and communication, but most were not dedicated full time to that activity. (The total FTEs outside the central unit equaled the size of my team.) Since this information is not normally close at hand at larger institutions, the results of surveys of staff size often vary greatly. However, there are some trends from which information might be gleaned and a few studies that attempt to quantify the staff size.

An obvious trend is that smaller institutions tend to have smaller staffs than larger ones. In its 2014 survey of nonprofit four-year institutions, the *Chronicle of Higher Education* reported that the average doctoral-granting university had close to 20 central staff, including 2.7 media/public relations staff, 2.4 graphic designers, 2.2 people in management/leadership positions, 1.8 in administrative support, 1.7 in web development/programming, 1.6 in copywriting, 1.3 in web content development, 1.1 in editing, 1 each in videography and project management, and a total of 4 FTEs in a range of other positions each less than 1 FTE. Master's-level colleges and baccalaureate colleges had teams that were concentrated in similar positions, though with fewer staff members (an average of 11 total FTEs at master's-level colleges and 10 at baccalaureate colleges).[30] It is worth noting that the report did not collect data on what functions the central unit served (e.g., marketing for admissions or alumni, website leadership) and did not include FTEs outside the central unit. A replication of this survey of CMOs in 2019 showed little change in the size of staffs compared with 2014, although a third said they had increased the number of employees in the last year.[31]

When asked what capacity they would add if they could make a strategic hire, a third or more of the CMOs responding in 2014 said they would hire a social media coordinator, a videographer, a market researcher, a copywriter, or a web content manager.[32] A year later, the CASE survey of trends indicated that a majority of chief marketing and communication officers reported that their resources had held steady or increased, so that if capacity were increased or reallocated, these were the areas of highest priority for hiring.[33] One might imagine that given the explosion of digital marketing, digital and content strategists might be among current priorities.

Polec's case study at four private institutions reported on the size of the central marketing and communication units but not on the staff in other units. These institutions' staffs ranged in size from 21 in the central unit at an institution of 4,000 students to 40 at an institution of 11,000 students. Polec recommended a measure by which institutions might report and compare at least their central staff: with a ratio of enrollment to central staff. At the four institutions, this ratio ranged from 153:1 at the smallest institution to 359:1 at the largest (13,300 enrolled).[34] Obviously, there is great variability in staff capacity relative to enrollment, probably a function of the variability in organizational structure.

During a recent consultation with a small college with an enrollment of nearly 800 students, I learned that the team included 10 FTEs, including the CMO, distributed across three units—

central marketing and communication, enrollment, and college advancement. A comparable college with an enrollment of 350 students had a team of 8 FTEs that included central marketing and communication and enrollment marketing. Both colleges outsourced some of their work to address capacity (photography and video in one instance, design in the other). The practice of outsourcing some functions was consistent with the data from the 2014 and 2019 CMO studies;[35] in 2019, 70 percent said they relied on freelancers.[36] The college with which I was consulting was preparing to undertake a major repositioning strategy, and the internal capacity was not sufficient to either design or maintain the associated branding work that would be necessary to implement the repositioning. So benchmarks, as scarce as they are in the practice of higher education marketing and communication, are not the only guide for establishing the right size of the organization. The nature of the work to be done and the strategic value to be built—enrollment and retention revenue, brand equity, and alumni support and engagement—should be considered in deciding what in-house or supplementary capacity is necessary.

Structural Complexity

One of the CMO's greatest ongoing challenges is how to manage, influence, and integrate the work of marketing and communication professionals who do not report to them. "Organizational structure is the biggest barrier to integrated marketing and branding on college campuses," observed Elizabeth Johnson, chairman of SimpsonScarborough.[37] The *Chronicle of Higher Education* reported that 30 percent of doctoral-granting institutions employ 20 or more marketers who do not report to the CMO, and 7 percent of those institutions have 100 or more. Three-quarters of master's-level institutions and baccalaureate colleges have marketers who work outside the central unit.[38]

Though leadership and management of resources to build value are most efficient and effective when responsibility and authority are streamlined and accountability is clear, it is nearly impossible in most institutions to function in an entirely centralized marketing and communication structure, given the nature of distributed authority and resources. The political capital it would take to reign in or reallocate resources—both human and financial—from distributed to central responsibility probably is not worth the cost. I followed the attempts at three large universities where the presidents saw the obvious waste and duplication, and supported or charged their CMOs with inventorying and centralizing hundreds of communicators and marketers. In all cases, leading such a process represented an existential threat for the CMO, and in two of the instances, it represented a crisis of confidence in the leadership.

Picking battles has its virtues, so this proposition represents a practical compromise: allowing for institutional variation, especially in size and type, as well as for changes that affect the professional practice of strategic integrated marketing, the structure should reflect responsibility and capacity at three levels—central, distributed, and shared.

Central Responsibility

In this category are functions that require or benefit strongly from institution-wide leadership and strategy. Commonly included in this category are responsibilities for leading or providing

- development of the institution's brand strategy, expression, and marketing plan
- advertising and media buying
- media and public relations
- issues management, crisis communication planning and response
- leadership positioning and communication

- communication for the launch of major institutional initiatives
- institutional publications (annual report and financial statements, president's report, alumni magazine, research publication, commencement program, etc.)
- digital marketing (organic and inbound marketing, paid search, paid social advertising)
- digital communication (including website design, content and user experience, social media)
- creative (including design, writing and editing, photography, video production)
- analytics and leadership for market research at an institution-wide level (including Google Analytics, measures of marketing return on investment, periodic stakeholder studies)

Which activities rise to the top of the priority list? Two-thirds or more of CMOs in 2014 said that they were primarily responsible for advertising, media/public relations, photography, media training, crisis communication, videography, and market research.[39] In 2019, the focus of the survey reflected choices that were more strategic, with 96 percent saying that strengthening and protecting their institution's reputation was a fundamental driver of their long-term goals.[40] Half or more said that they were involved in the marketing of individual colleges and schools (91%), recruitment strategy (86%), student experience (63%), diversity and inclusion initiatives (63%), employee morale (56%), alumni relations strategy (55%), fundraising strategy (53%), and program or product development (51%).[41] A CASE survey of communication and marketing trends showed that in 2015 the activities that took up more of the CMOs' time than any other included constituent communication, as well as branding and strategic considerations.[42]

Larger institutions may have the resources to build the capacity for these central functions in-house, while smaller institutions may have to outsource some of these functions to agencies or freelancers. Even large institutions may outsource functions that are needed periodically but not continuously, such as market research, or very specialized functions, such as media buying; these can be done as a fee for service or on a retainer.

Distributed Responsibility

In institutions with highly distributed responsibility and authority, executives throughout the organization often develop and staff their own communication capacity so that it is dedicated exclusively to their priorities. In smaller, more centralized institutions, the central communication and marketing unit may provide the services through an in-house agency model, serving the various units as their clients, as capacity allows. In most organizations, large and small, with clear strategic priorities and limited resources, it is not possible for the central unit to perform every desired communication and marketing function, nor should they. Yet these functions must be tended in order to garner attendance, sell tickets, or tell a story of a particular individual or program that is critically important at a "local" or unit level, even when it doesn't rise to the level of institutional priority. These distributed activities often address the following functions:

- academic unit communication (schools or colleges, departments, centers, etc.)
- alumni communication
- athletic marketing, sports information, and sponsorships
- arts marketing (for performing arts, museum exhibits, etc.)
- community relations
- government and legislative relations
- special events

In the 2014 *Chronicle* survey, more than half the CMOs said they played "some role" even when responsibilities were distributed, including work on commencement and major campus events, alumni and fundraising events, recruitment events, and new-student orientation.[43] In other activities, they may play no role at all. Tools for coordinating, integrating, and influencing activities performed outside the central marketing and communication office are suggested.

Shared Responsibilities

Many institutions distribute responsibility and authority for key initiatives to leaders among the executive team and academic leadership, who possess professional and subject expertise and who require marketing and communication tools to achieve their goals. For activities including enrollment marketing and development communication, the structure should provide the CMO with some means to influence the work directly at a strategic and tactical level, with outcomes enhanced through strategic integrated marketing to cultivate exchanges of value with audiences (students, families, and donors) whose engagement and support builds value for the institution. Such shared responsibilities may include the following:

- enrollment marketing, undergraduate and graduate
- development communication (fundraising, stewardship, annual fund)
- brand integration with unit-level communication
- media relationships with reporters and editors
- constituent communication (alumni, internal audiences)
- internal communication

The structure should allow for sharing responsibility with the executives responsible for advancement and enrollment. Matrix management with dotted-line responsibility to one or both executives and shared responsibility for performance management and compensation constitute one option. This model is used more frequently in the advancement functions of development and alumni relations, and theoretically it should apply to the work of marketing and communication. Practically speaking, it takes commitment and a lot of work for executive team members to sustain healthy working relationships with those in the matrixed roles.

Another structural alternative, advocated by Larry Lauer[44] and first instituted by him at Texas Christian University, is an account executive model, in which central marketing staff are assigned responsibility for working with their counterparts in the units as strategic partners, not simply as order takers or service providers. This model has been replicated at a number of institutions. American University adopted this approach, with members of the marketing team assigned to undergraduate admissions, development, and alumni relations and to the schools and colleges for their graduate marketing functions. The marketing team member became the central team expert on the goals, initiatives, and plans for their assigned units and provided strategy and central resources for tactical execution.

Embedding staff in the work of other units with shared marketing and communication responsibilities allows the central team members to gain a deeper understanding of the business objectives and challenges for the respective units. This also ensures a measure of influence on the quality of the marketing outcomes and opportunities to coordinate and integrate it with the institution's overarching brand strategy. In addition, this allows for focus on strategic goals that can benefit from marketing expertise to build value. The account executive assignments to these units do not relieve the CMO and executive counterparts from regular and consistent coordination related to goal setting and relationship building, but they do provide a means for operational execution on a frequent and consistent basis.

It is worth noting that all of these structural options provide the CMO a measure of bureaucratic power to effect change and build value, but none are sufficient. Support from the president and the executive team are necessary to develop effective, sustainable hybrid structures. In addition, the CMO must develop significant network power, through relationship-building, connecting, the use of data and analytics, and transformational leadership; otherwise, the structure alone won't ensure effective execution.[45]

Tools for Integration in a Complex Structure

If responsibility and authority for marketing and communication is distributed or shared, organizational devices can help to develop shared expectations, leverage investments, and increase buy-in and support for shared goals. The CMO is the institution's chief officer for this work and should be positioned to provide strategic integrated marketing leadership for all of the efforts, whether they are executed centrally or at a unit level. One way to reinforce this position is for the CMO to establish a marketing task force and working groups or steering committees to gather professionals from across the campus to align their work and share responsibility and accountability for brand integration in marketing communication at the unit level.

Marketing Task Force

A college or university marketing task force, charged by the president and chaired by the CMO, is an excellent tool for developing buy-in and gathering input for major marketing initiatives. In the 2019 CMO survey, 59 percent said that they met regularly with such a group.[46] This group should be the most informed group of participants in any marketing effort, and their role should be advisory; that is, they should make recommendations to the institution's leadership, who are the decision-makers. They should operate in a manner that achieves consensus, so that all support the group's final recommendations.

The projects the marketing task force guides should be high-level marketing initiatives—guiding market research to form a brand strategy, development of the strategy, and creative expression of the brand strategy in tools like campaigns, slogans, tag-lines, and logo systems. They should help set measures of effectiveness and monitor outcomes at least annually. They should be among the first to recognize and call for adjustments to strategy or refreshment of the creative expression.

The membership should include high-level representatives of various units representing important constituencies that are key to marketing plans and outcomes. Admissions, athletics, alumni, development, and student affairs should all be represented by senior managers who commit to exchanging information with their home units and leadership and bringing back input from their departments or divisions. A representative of the CFO's office can help shape expectations for resources, and a representative of the institutional research and assessment office can help share data or shape data collection. (Both can serve as resources to the task force, if not members.) Depending on the institutional context and strategic priorities, a representative of the government relations unit or those who develop and promote the institution's research agenda could be important contributors. One or two academic leaders (deans) who help shape opinion are a must, as are faculty representatives—opinion leaders and those with expertise in marketing, market research, and communication are great contributors. One or two communication and marketing professionals from outside the central unit who command respect or have strong related experience should be included. Representatives of staff, including HR or an elected staff council, are helpful. Student representation is also a must, and student leaders or those in related degree programs are best able to contribute in meaningful ways. Finally, members of the CMO's senior management who supervise key areas—communication and media, marketing, creative services, and digital—should be members as well.

Ideally the group would be large enough to be representative but small enough to move nimbly and make recommendations. Members should be appointed for annual, renewable terms and agree to come not just to represent their constituencies or mind parochial concerns but to wear their broad institutional "hats" and keep the greater good of the institution at the forefront of every decision. Ultimately, this group extends advocacy for marketing efforts beyond the central office to every corner of the campus community.

The president and the CMO can reinforce the importance of this work by sharing a short annual report from the task force to the president, and the president should provide a formal response with acknowledgments, encouragement, and a list of future challenges to consider.

Working Groups

Institutional leaders can encourage staff who do not report to the same executive but play similar roles to come together periodically as groups with shared interests. Members benefit individually, and the institution benefits from greater levels of integration. A campus communicators group, for example, might be convened by the CMO or by member of the team who is primarily responsible for communication and media. Such a group can establish procedures and processes to make sure that relationships with reporters are cultivated by one primary staff contact, so that, for example, two or more institutional representatives do not contact the same reporter at the same time or on the same topic. They can also establish practices to coordinate on approaches to opinion editors, who expect the institution to offer one op-ed submission (not several from competing experts) and to treat the content as exclusive to that news outlet (not offered to several outlets simultaneously—a big no-no). They might meet monthly to focus on a topic (developing policies and procedures for media on campus, sharing tools to target media and distribute releases, media monitoring, measuring impact) or benefit from professional development (developing content strategy, working with faculty, developing relationships with reporters, producers, and editors, etc.) They might also use tools to coordinate with one another, reduce duplicative efforts, and leverage work around shared interests with short, 30-minute calls at the beginning of each week to swap notes on their priorities.

Steering Committees

Small groups of interested stakeholders can help develop and reinforce policies, procedures, and processes that govern shared communication resources. For example, if the institution possesses or needs governance to support effective and proper use of its web content management system and the institutional content hosted on it, a group that represents academic, administrative, technical, and communication interests can develop policies, recommend priorities, ensure that training and compliance resources are in place, stimulate innovation, and support resource development. A college or university's trademark and licensing program is another important component of brand management that may benefit from a steering committee comprising representatives from athletics, auxiliary services, campus retail operations, procurement, and the general counsel's office. The president and the executive team should consider carefully who should lead these committees, and to whom they should report.

The CMO as Internal Consultant and Air Traffic Controller

With regard to responsibilities for which everyone is responsible and no one is accountable, the CMO or designee can be assigned to consult, advise, approve, and coordinate. Constituent communication and a subset, internal communication, often fall into this category. Many parts of an institution have business reasons to communicate with a particular constituency, as well as to all faculty, staff, and students in certain situations. These offices should not be unduly restrained, but they might be guided in terms of content, frequency, channel, and effectiveness by a CMO who has become fully integrated with and conversant with all aspects of the institution.

Often the CMO takes the lead in establishing regular and high-level internal communication, and the CMO should always be in the lead for crisis communication (which is a centrally led function, not a shared one, as noted above). But CMOs can also provide templates, offer writing or editing support to their colleagues in other units, and coordinate editorial calendars for scheduling frequent institutional communications so that they don't all land at one time or at inappropriate times (e.g., in a crisis). Some institutional leaders insist that all campus-wide communication be approved by the CMO. CMOs may also develop policies regarding the use of internal communication tools (mass campus emails, institutional social media channels, the intranet or portal, newsletters, etc.).

Many institutions that recognize the power of an informed and satisfied workforce struggle with how best to lead internal communication strategically. Models like corporate communication may offer some value, but given the distribution of authority among many autonomous units, it may have its limits. Suffice to say that many of my colleagues are struggling with how to effectively manage internal communication in the context of higher education.

Assessing Organizational Capacity

Presidents and executive teams may find themselves at a crossroads. To build revenue, goodwill, support, loyalty, and reputation, they may take a sharp turn in strategy or seek to communicate about the institution in ambitious ways that they haven't imagined previously.

This chapter shows that while there are few benchmarks, there are some strategies for assessing what currently exists and what might need adjustment. One common way to start is to hire a strong CMO and assign a thorough but prompt assessment as the first order of business. The CMO can rely on staff annual goals and performance assessments and meet with and interview key members the central team, as well as colleagues, who hold a perspective on the strengths and limits of the group. CMOs can audit the existing work products that the team produces for evidence of strategy, integration, and effectiveness. They can review budgets and staffing levels, as well as capacities, and compare them with those in the 2014 and 2019 studies of CMOs.[47] In addition, CASE maintains a management checklist for every area of advancement practice, including marketing and communication, which CMOs can use to evaluate and compare the practices, tools, and systems currently in place as well as those that might be needed in the future.[48]

To return to a theme of this book, the organization must use its capabilities and expertise to address the strategic work to be accomplished. The existing structure and resources may be sufficient to maintain a current institutional position in the marketplace, but if the leadership anticipates the introduction of a major new initiative or if the current team is consistently demonstrating inadequate performance in certain areas, adjustments will be needed. It should not take more than three months to do a thorough assessment and shape recommendations for a plan to adjust. This is particularly appropriate in the early tenure of a new CMO or upon the arrival of a new president, when adjustments might be mandated by preferences or new strategic priorities.

If there is no CMO, or if the leadership is losing confidence in the current CMO's ability to assess, adjust, and perform, an outside consultant might be appropriate. I know from experience as both a consultant and a CMO leading the organization to be assessed how threatening and anxiety-producing this process can be. Therefore, the consultant should be an experienced, respected leader in the field who operates with compassion and discretion. To avoid a conflict of interest, I would strongly urge that it be made clear that the consultant cannot become a candidate for the CMO role if the assessment leads to an opening.

To find an external consultant to perform such an assessment, an institution can seek recommendations from respected CMOs or from agency leaders with whom the institution has an existing relationship. An excellent resource, if time allows, is the the Registry for College and University Presidents,[49] which will identify an interim communication and marketing executive, whose full-time responsibility for an interim period (6-12 months) would be to keep the trains running, do the assessment, and even guide the search for the next CMO. (Again, to avoid a potential conflict of interest, the interim appointee cannot be considered for the permanent appointment.)

Now that we have framed the work of strategic integrated marketing in the context of its purpose to build value, defined the key terms, and reviewed the terrain of leadership and organizational assessment, we turn to the substance of marketing and branding, viewed through the lens of the president, the executive team, and the trustees, who must have at least a discerning consumer's knowledge of what they are investing in so that they can properly set expectations, provide resources, and measure the effectiveness and return on investment. The place to start in marketing—always—is the laying of the foundation of strategy through market research.

Key Questions for Leaders and Their CMOs

- How does the president demonstrate support for the strategic value of marketing and communication?

- Does the CMO have a seat at the table for institutional strategy conversations, and does the reporting structure support the CMO's success?

- Is our marketing and communication team structured appropriately? Do we have the right balance of central responsibility and distributed responsibility, given our institutional context?

Chapter 3

The Foundation

----

*Market Research to Assess the Current Brand
and Set Goals*

Diligent, accurate and timely research is indispensable for two
reasons: First, you are not your customers. Second, everything
changes.
—Thomas Hayes, dean, Williams College of Business, Xavier University

One of the biggest changes I have seen in my time as a higher
education marketer is the attitude toward research as a fundamental requirement for the formation and refinement of strategy. Earlier in my career, it was uncommon for leaders to willingly invest in brand research to understand their institution's
position in the market relative to competitors, learn the attitudes
and perceptions of key audiences, or test the response to various
strategic alternatives. More often than not, leaders who did want
to invest in strategic integrated marketing wanted to get right to
it: they preferred not to spend time and money on research and
jumped directly to shaping messages and developing the plans
to deliver them. However, as Robert Sevier points out, "Any
marketing plan that does not include research at its base is almost surely flawed. It either will fail or will take more time and
money to execute."[1]

Sometimes leaders are loath to do this research as the foundation of institutional strategy, fearing that no matter what intelli-

gence they might gain, they would create the unacceptable impression that they are allowing students to drive academic decisions about what institutions will do and how. Thomas Hayes surmised that institutions' resistance to market research might be due to "a pervasive sense among many in the field of higher education that they simply know what students, parents, alumni and donors are looking for."[2]

It has always struck me as ironic that academic institutions, beacons of rigorous methods of scholarship in the pursuit of truth and dissemination of knowledge, were not inclined to recognize the value of starting with *market research*, which is defined by Sevier as the "systematic design, collection, analysis and reporting of data and findings relevant to a specific marketing situation an institution faces."[3] Hayes, recognizing the inconsistency of faculty and administrators' accepting the importance of research to discover truth in their own academic disciplines yet not appreciating the value of research in the field of marketing, cautioned them against relying on personal assumptions: "On many college campuses, the spirit of research in pursuit of knowledge did not carry over into the institution's own strategic decision making. . . . Prejudice and assumption in the absence of research succeed only in clouding decision making and impeding the formulation of effective strategic initiatives. Diligent, accurate and timely research is indispensable for two reasons: First, you are not your customers. Second, everything changes."[4]

One of my favorite exercises to remind leaders of this wisdom is to put two creative concepts for a recruitment video, brochure, website, or campaign in front of the executive team after the concept has been through creative testing with the target audience. If I ask the leaders (average age near 60 years, often mostly white, and male) which they prefer, they inevitably choose the concept that the target audience (average age 17 and diverse in both age and gender) did not. This exercise has never failed. Not once. A provost I once worked with joked that in the future we could avoid the time and expense of creative testing and just go with the version he did not pick!

As higher education marketing has come of age, the field has matured, the tools have improved, and the value of market research has become more evident. Perhaps contributing to its greater acceptance may be the intense competition and the advent of an era marked by the rise of data and analytics to assess and measure performance. No matter what contributed to greater recognition of the importance of this foundation, I'm grateful that more leaders have embraced it.

Robert Sevier identifies five primary ways that market research can help leaders:

1. Provide perceptual data from key audiences, who act based on their perceptions. Understanding how an institution is perceived or misperceived is critical to making decisions about strategy, as well as influencing or motivating behaviors that build value.
2. Suggest which strategic alternatives are most likely to be preferred by and motivating to stakeholders.
3. Clarify and set priorities, for example, regarding which audiences to focus on, or which options are likely to provide the greatest return in the shortest amount of time.
4. Test ideas and creative approaches, such as designs, logos, campaign concepts, names, etc. This kind of research is invaluable for making adjustments and avoiding mistakes.
5. Monitor the institution's competitive environment for problems or opportunities.[5]

The primary focus of this chapter is market research to establish or refine an institution's brand strategy, which encompasses many of the purposes listed above. Keep in mind that every institution has a brand, and it exists in the minds of its stakeholders. Engaging in a process of research to understand what those stakeholders know, think of, and feel about the institution is the first step in developing a strategy to influence and manage that brand to advance strategic goals. For institutions engaging in market research for the first time, the results will lay down a foundation for a long-lasting strategy. Others are seeking to understand how to adjust their brand strategy as they make progress toward goals, experience changes in their competitive market (as a result of changes in their own institutions or of disruptive moves by competitors), consider new directions under new leadership, or anticipate and adapt to changes in their traditional audience segments.

Later in this chapter, market research for purposes other than brand building, including research on market demand, pricing studies, and research to address a very narrow problem or issue, is covered briefly. In addition, the value of secondary sources of data (research collected for another purpose, not specifically related to the research purpose, e.g., brand strategy) is reviewed.

Market Research to Establish or Renew Brand Strategy

Why should college and university leaders concern themselves with market research? They aren't usually the ones responsible for driving the process of researching, shaping, or refining the brand—that's the CMO's job—so they don't need detailed knowledge of methodology and analysis, though those leaders who come from scholarly backgrounds, particularly social scientists, will have expertise and special interest. Rather, leaders need to have confidence in the research they fund. They can interpret the results and ultimately use them to make decisions about strategy. In addition, they care deeply about the questions various audiences will be asked about their institution, so they have an important stake in what is studied and how. Becoming an educated consumer of market research will help them ensure that their institutions avoid common mistakes at this stage of the process, discussed below.

Building or reshaping a brand strategy should always start with brand research. As Sevier stated, "Solid marketing plans rest on a foundation of research."[6] Research will provide the discipline that guides the major goals the brand strategy will address and the requirements that direct the creative expression of the brand. Further, research will ultimately inform content strategy and messages for key audiences. Elizabeth Johnson, of SimpsonScarborough, a nationally recognized expert in the use of research to drive marketing and branding efforts, advises that "research is the foundation for your long-term brand strategy, and the insurance policy that protects it along the way."[7]

Johnson, who counts hundreds of colleges and universities among her firm's clients, is familiar with the inclination of institutions to change their messages frequently, because internal audiences get bored and tired of using them or because a new leader arrives and wants to put a fresh spin on messages to mark a new era. She likes to remind leaders that investing in a brand strategy is a long-term commitment. It takes time for audiences to develop awareness, support, and loyalty, because it requires changes in long-held perceptions that drive human behavior. "The research protects the strategy as you go and it gives you that touchstone you can always go back to and say no, this is why we're doing it this way. This is why our position is what it is. This is why we're messaging that way." She references American University's process of using three stakeholder studies over ten years to shape, measure, and refine the brand strategy as an example of research to inform and protect the brand strategy as it grows.

Moreover, in what would have been considered radical even ten years ago, Johnson increasingly finds herself talking with presidents and boards about how brand research should be part of the strategic planning process. "That's where it fits. I don't know how any institution can be talking about mission, vision, and goals without understanding how they are perceived by internal and external audiences." Recently, a new president was so keen to build market research into his early tenure that he met with Johnson after his appointment was announced and signed a contract for the research to inform institutional and brand strategy on his first day in office.

Since strategic integrated marketing is a process for building value, such enlightened approaches to market research as a part of strategic planning are likely to be more common in the future. Johnson attributes the shift in leaders' attitudes to market forces desensitizing people to the academic concern that customer focus would have too much influence on strategy. "Even highly selective institutions with healthy brands, who aren't desperate for students" are using market research to develop, refine, or measure their strategy. She shared three examples of current clients: the University of California, Los Angeles, is using research to track brand health over time; the University of North Carolina is using research to segment its alumni audiences; and New York University is using research to craft a brand narrative that fits the entire university, one that encompasses 11 schools as well as campuses around the world.

So, institutions with brands that are weak or strong, well managed or unmanaged, recognize that research is the place to begin in building or refining brand strategy to build value over time. Who leads and guides the work, how the scope of the research is shaped, and how to build support from important constituencies are the next considerations.

Roles and Responsibilities in Brand Research

CMO, President, Cabinet, and Board

The CMO should guide the development of the market research to shape brand strategy. If the institution recognizes the importance of the findings to shaping strategic goals, the CMO will need to work closely with the executive team, who certainly will be pivotally involved in strategic planning and who should also decide on any brand strategy (a management decision). The board can offer insights and avoid blind spots.

Since completing the market research is the first phase of a larger process to develop or refine the institution's brand, decision-makers and advisors should be involved at the earliest stages. I've advised CMOs to bring leaders along because they can't expect their buy-in, trust, and willingness to take reasonable risks to differentiate if the leaders weren't involved in the journey to reach those decisions. It is important for leaders to be informed, updated, and ready to provide input and guidance at key milestones.

Johnson identifies a side benefit of this involvement: it builds the president's and the CMO's credibility with the board during the process. She describes the impact at a small college in the Midwest with whose board she has had four meetings, arranged by the president and the CMO, over a period of one year: "The credibility that the president and the marketing department have with the board has increased twentyfold, just by going through the research project, the development of the brand platform, then going through the creative concepts, showing them the two concepts, and then showing them the results of the concept test."

As a result, when the time came for implementation and the board needed to authorize the expenditure of resources that exceeded the authority of the president alone, "They literally doubled their budget, and there's no way they would have done that without building, without going through that whole process of the research. The board says, 'These people know what they're doing. They know what their audiences want. This completely aligns with everything I believe about the institution. What do you need?'"

Internal or External Research Experts

A number of times during the process of developing or refining a brand strategy, it will be necessary to decide whether to rely on internal capacity or to get outside help. The beginning of the process is certainly one of those times. Depending on the expertise and maturity of a college or university's marketing organization and institutional research assets and priorities, this may be the time to go outside for help.

There are CMOs who have expertise in market research, but for the ones who don't, getting some expert help is a good idea. Moreover, the CMO is like the quarterback for the entire process, guiding the input and involvement of various constituencies and leaders along the way, in addition to all the other aspects of the job. Progress on the research is fundamental to everything that follows, and it should not slow down every time a media issue or campus controversy requires the CMO's undivided attention.

The institutional research office may be a terrific resource. The staff have access to the institution's data, which they probably understand better than anyone. They are often familiar with the research methods that will be employed in brand research. However, institutional assessment and brand research are different areas of expertise. Moreover, firms that conduct market research for brand development have economies of scale that allow them to do the work faster and more efficiently. They know the questions, the challenges, and the appropriate methods to achieve given purposes. They already know how best to reach various audiences if they have done so at other institutions. And finally, if the institutional research office is already weighed down with annual research priorities (new student census, climate surveys, administration of the National Survey of Student Engagement or other national instruments, graduate census, etc.) or periodic priorities (assessment and self-study for periodic accreditation), the brand research might be shortchanged.

This is no time to try to substitute data the institution already possesses for applied market research to build the brand, measure progress, or refine it. The findings from an admitted student survey might provide a window into market segments of one stakeholder group (admitted prospective undergraduate students), but it is not brand research. An institution should build or refine its brand based on recent data collected and analyzed for that specific purpose.

If the institution decides it needs outside help, the question arises, which kind of firm is best? As their marketing planning has developed, some institutions have relied on marketing, advertising, or public relations agencies with whom they have an existing contract or relationship. These firms may have in-house market research capability, or they may subcontract for it when their clients need it. If an agency has this capability, already knows the institution, and is trusted by the institution's leaders, this could be a fine option. Even if the institution does not have an existing agency relationship, it may be preferable to have a full-service firm handle the whole branding process—research, development of strategy and creative expression, implementation and monitoring.

The field of higher education marketing has developed to the point that there are a number of good firms that specialize in higher education marketing and branding. These firms will often have a leg up in terms of understanding and respecting the academic culture, as well as the process of vetting, consensus-building, and decision-making that is distinct to colleges and universities. (If the understanding and respect for higher education culture and organization are not evident in the firm's leadership and business development staff or in their references, then run, do not walk, to find a firm that not only understands but appreciates and loves higher education. There are plenty of good ones, some of whom are mentioned in this book. The principals of many of these firms are among the leading professionals in higher education marketing.)

If an institution is worried about proximity or regional preferences or constraints, such firms often have multiple offices or employees working remotely across the country. If not, they will build into their price estimate the cost of planned travel and offer remote meeting options through technology that close the distance.

An institution might hire one of these firms, or it might hire one that specializes only in market research to handle only the research and resulting implications for strategy. Sometimes the firms that excel in creative expression of the brand are not as strong in research or strategy, and vice versa. Parsing the effort into separate areas of work allows an institution to choose the best partner at each step. On the other hand, a firm that appears to fit the institution's needs at one stage might offer a financial incentive for hiring the firm for all the stages.

Finally, there may be local firms that know the institution and its primary markets quite well; hiring one of them might be good for both the institution and the community. With the caveat that it is always best to find a firm that knows and appreciates higher education, this might be a good option.

This is no time for pro bono work by a firm that is connected to a trustee. The relationship with a partner should be free of potential conflicts, and an institution should be certain that it will have the focused attention of the firm's talent, which always goes to paying clients first. If it turns out that the relationship with the firm sours and it needs to end, the decision won't be complicated by other concerns.

Stakeholders as Participants

Chapter 2 includes the recommendation to develop a marketing task force to be led by the CMO and appointed by the president. This group's primary purpose would be to guide major marketing initiatives, including the development or refinement of brand strategy, beginning with brand research. I like to think of this group as the most informed participants in the process. They collectively represent the perspectives of all the key stakeholders, they offer expertise in shaping or interpreting the research, and they will serve as its primary advocates when the findings and resulting recommendations are shared with the community. (For the makeup of such a task force, see chapter 2.)

The marketing task force's responsibility is to steer or guide the work and make recommendations, not to make final decisions. They can help to develop the scope of work and, if appropriate, interview prospective firms and weigh in on recommendations. When the decision about research capacity and expertise has been made, their role is to work with the CMO and the research expert or firm to hone the research questions, help gather the stakeholder data and identify subjects in the populations or samples to be studied, monitor the response rates and consider adjustments as necessary, and develop the analysis and the findings that will shape the strategy. (Later they will guide the strategy development as well.) They will support the presentation of the key findings to the campus community, the leadership, the alumni board, and the governing board so that maximum input, awareness, and buy-in are achieved. They will commend the major research findings to the executive team, who might accept the recommendations, ask for clarifications, or propose modifications. The CMO should make sure that it all comes together and that everyone plays their role.

The Campus Community

It is wise to involve faculty, staff, and students at the earliest stages of the branding process and to keep them informed along the way. Providing opportunities to participate in the process by providing individual input can be the first step in building awareness and credibility for the entire effort. It may be helpful for the president and the CMO to frame the process first, translating marketing terms into language that is more common in academic communities. For example, one might preface the launch of the brand research as a data-driven basis for shaping strategy and more effectively telling the institution's story.

If time and budget allow, broaden participation in the research phase of the process by inviting the campus community to provide their perspectives. A census of the entire population of current students, faculty, staff, and alumni is more cost effective than it has ever been, thanks to online surveys. Even a sample that represents a significant proportion of a stakeholder group can widen awareness and participation. Focus groups made up of influencers and leaders to help discover current brand associations and differentiators allow the institution to hear from representatives of its closest constituents. When the research findings are presented, it is wise to remind the community of all the opportunities they had to participate.

Crafting an Effective Scope of Work

The scope of work to be accomplished in the research phase of the branding process can vary by purpose, time, and money.

Purpose

An institution that does not currently have a brand strategy will necessarily have more to do. It will need to understand how it is perceived by key audiences relative to market competitors and in relation to specific strategic goals (enrollment, fundraising, etc.). It will need to determine how aware various audiences are of the institution as well as their level of familiarity with it and competitors. The institution will need to ascertain current brand associations, both positive and negative (e.g., affordable value, high-quality academics, party school, a reputation for frequent racist incidents), and how widely they are known and held. It will need to identify potential differentiators (from competitors) and test how authentic, relevant, and motivating they are to various stakeholders so that it can develop a distinctive value proposition. It might want to test strategic alternatives under consideration in order to determine which to emphasize or how to communicate about them. The institution will want to know which audiences or segments are its biggest promoters and which are the biggest detractors so that the brand strategy can establish audience priorities. (It is a rare institution that has the budget and resources to effectively address all its stakeholders at once in the deployment of a brand strategy; better to make choices informed by data.)

Leaders whose institutions fall into the category of getting started on a first brand strategy should be assured that even though the scope of the research will be bigger than for those who have been intentionally branding their institution for some time, it has other inherent value beyond the shaping of the first strategy. First, it will set benchmarks against which progress can be measured, and second, it is an excellent means for convening members of an academic community to consider how it will represent itself, starting with data rather than with personal experience or opinion. It will provide opportunities for stakeholder awareness, learning, and buy-in for the branding process that cannot be replicated through other means. When done well, market research builds credibility for those leading the process and confidence in the ultimate outcomes.

By contrast, for an institution that has an established brand strategy and is looking at what progress has been made or what adjustments might be needed, the purpose of the research is not as broad, so the scope of the research may be smaller. While there may be questions that should be replicated (because they measure change), all the questions related to discovery are no longer as relevant. The research process becomes more honed and efficient the further along in the branding process an institution is. Of course, if something significant has occurred or developed since the brand strategy was first established, the value of addressing that should be explored.

Specific research methods lend themselves better to some purposes than to others and may be more or less costly in terms of data gathering and analysis. *Qualitative methods* provide rich accounts in the voices of audiences that help an institution home in on its defining characteristics, strengths and weaknesses, brand associations, and differentiators, and they elicit the language constituents use to describe them. For institutions trying to discover and identify aspects of a potential brand strategy, this method is crucial. Focus groups and interviews are two forms of qualitative research that are often easier and quicker to get in the field. The analysis can be lengthy (with such a lot of unstructured data to categorize and analyze), and it can be more costly than some forms of quantitative research. The results of qualitative methods may provide themes, but they do not measure magnitude, and one cannot say with reliability and confidence that the findings represent the entire audience of interest.

Quantitative methods measure a phenomenon of interest (e.g., a perception or behavior) using a statistically valid and randomly generated sample to represent a larger population, or they attempt to reach an entire population and invest serious effort in generating high response rates, or they use statistical methods to limit non-response bias. Analysis of quantitative methods may be more rapid than analysis of qualitative methods. Surveys are the most common instrument of quantitative research. Online surveys delivered through email and text may be the easiest and least costly to administer, but they depend on good institutional data to reach the targeted subjects, along with incentives and targeted follow-up to generate sufficient response.

A college or university will have scholars experienced in both types of research methods. A strong rationale for the choice of methods based on the purpose of the research will be compelling to these scholars. Johnson emphasizes the power of data—especially quantitative data that measure and are generalizable—

to garner the respect of faculty whose everyday roles include research.

Certain methods lend themselves better than others to particular audiences or circumstances. Reaching executive leaders in business, government, or higher education may require interviews, because surveys are likely to be delegated to staffers, whose perspective is not what is desired. For institutions just starting to develop a brand strategy, when the institution needs to discover or uncover aspects of the brand that will be compelling to stakeholders, a mix of qualitative and quantitative methods provides the best outcomes. Focus groups and interviews allow themes to emerge in the language of key audiences, which can then be used to test the brand's relevance and relative power to engage and motivate stakeholders to act in ways that will support the institution. For institutions that have had a strategy in place for some time and are looking to refine it, quantitative methods alone may be sufficient.

At American University, for example, our first stakeholder study began with interviews with 90 faculty, staff, and alumni leaders. These yielded nine possible positioning statements, which were further honed and tested in surveys. The sequence allowed us to reveal a small number of relevant and motivating positions, along with key descriptors of the institution's personality, character, strengths, and weaknesses, its position relative to competitors, and its relative familiarity and favorability among various audiences. All of this input went into the development of a brand platform that included a final positioning statement, tone, personality, and statements that triggered maximum positive response from various audiences.

Even then, when the marketing task force at American University felt confident about the positioning it was about to recommend—a combination of both the "mirror," reflecting who we were, and the "bridge," reflecting what we aspired to be—the provost felt that it did not adequately capture the aspirations for the future related to academic excellence, which were key to the university's strategic plans. The president agreed. Our research consultant, Johnson, met with the three of us and agreed that we should pause and explore an adjustment. She proposed that we interview 15 of our highest-profile scholars—another qualitative method—to hear their views of the institution and get their reaction to the draft positioning.

This second round of interviews made a real difference. Though the draft positioning resonated well with these influential faculty, they suggested and emphasized slight adjustments that pulled it closer to the core academic purpose of the institution. Our next draft had the support of both the provost and the president. It was better for the adjustment and we had the leadership buy-in we needed. Also, a dozen influential faculty were willing to embrace the final result and support it because they had participated in the process.

Many scholars know that the sequence qualitative-quantitative-qualitative produces exceptional results, but it does take more time. In this instance, the extra month we took to conduct those interviews spared us significant resistance that we might have faced later had we not stopped to do more interviews and make refinements.

The second and third iterations of the stakeholder study, at intervals of three and five years, respectively, were limited exclusively to quantitative methods, and we were able to reduce the scope of work because we were replicating questions we had asked previously.

Time and Money

Market researchers can produce results fast or slowly, at low or greater expense. Johnson tells clients to think of the research scope as being like an accordion. It can be as small or as large as time and resources allow. She provided an example of a tool that her firm provides to clients (table 1) to help them navigate the choices based on available resources and time demands.

TABLE 1. *Sample scope of work for research*

Target audience	Method	Very small	Small	Medium	Large	Very large
Prospective traditional undergrads	20 in-depth interviews			X	X	X
	Online survey (n = 400)	X	X	X	X	X
Prospective grad/adult students	20 in-depth interviews					X
	Online survey (n = 400)			X	X	X
Alumni and donors	2 online focus groups					X
	Online survey (n = 400)	X	X	X	X	X
Parents of prospective traditional undergrads	20 in-depth interviews			X	X	X
	Online survey (n = 400)					X
High-school guidance counselors and community-college transfer coordinators	20 in-depth interviews		X	X	X	X
	Online survey (n = 400)			X	X	X
Business and community leaders	20 in-depth interviews		X	X	X	X
	Online survey (n = 400)				X	X
Higher education peer faculty and administration	20 in-depth interviews		X	X	X	X
	Online survey (n = 400)				X	X
Internal audiences (faculty, staff, current students)	2 in-person focus groups with faculty					X
	2 in-person focus groups with undergrads				X	X
	2 in-person focus groups with grad students					X
	Online survey (n = 1,100)	X	X	X	X	X

Source: SimpsonScarborough.

The research experts, whether an outside firm or internal staff, should guide the CMO and the marketing task force through the various options available according to purpose, time, and money. It is the responsibility of the CMO to navigate these choices with leaders to determine what will be most relevant to the goals of the institution and the development or refinement of the brand.

Determining What to Study

The role of college and university leaders is not to be down in the weeds on developing survey items. However, there should be basic agreement between the CMO, the president, and the executive team on what goals the research is designed to address and which audiences should be included. To the extent that these decisions drive time and costs, the CMO should be negotiating with the leadership about what is needed. The research experts (either internal or at the firm being used), with the help of the task force, will decide on appropriate areas of study and methods, aligned with appropriate questions, based on the goals.

The leadership should not be surprised by the purpose, method, and areas of inquiry. Leaders may be particularly sensitive about how a topic is addressed in a question, so a review by the president and the executive team before the instruments or interview scripts are final is always a good idea. For example, characteristics or attributes of the college or university are likely to be sought out or tested, and the leadership should be satisfied with the language used. The CMO should negotiate any leadership concerns and make sure they are addressed by the research experts, while maintaining the integrity and purpose of the study.

Vetting the Results, the Analysis, and the Findings

In keeping with the counsel provided above, it is wise for the CMO and the marketing task force to check in with leaders at key milestones in this process. One of those milestones is when the data are in and have been analyzed and the CMO and the marketing task force have taken a first good pass with the research experts at interpreting the findings and made them presentable for others. The president and the executive team should be the first to see the findings and to get details on the specific data and analysis, if so desired. It should be the responsibility of the CMO and the research expert to explicitly present any potentially sensitive results to the leadership before the findings are more widely shared and acted upon.

Leaders should be encouraged to help interpret the findings. Then the results may be more widely shared by the CMO, the researchers, and the task force with constituency leaders and the board, at least in a summary form, so that all whose buy-in is needed view the steps in the branding process as following logically and reasonably.

Leaders should decide how widely and publicly to share the results. Transparency and participation usually benefit the process, but keep in mind that the results represent proprietary information about competitive advantages and disadvantages. For that reason, it may make sense to control access to or distribution of the findings using technology tools.

Avoiding Common Mistakes

Leaders can learn from the mistakes of others. Here are five ways to avoid mistakes that could limit the findings and the effectiveness of the resulting brand strategy:

Ask the Hard Questions

In order to know and understand what stakeholders think about the institution, one must ask. Leaders who are afraid to explore the existence or magnitude of a suspected negative perception, such as whether the university is perceived as a party school or whether a controversy covered in the press has left a lasting impression of the college, are flying blind when they get around to building the brand strategy. If an issue presents a challenge for one or more key audiences, leaders need to know so that they can figure out what to do about it (and not just in the brand strategy). Moreover, sometimes leaders think something is an issue when in fact it is not or when it is only an issue for one segment or audience. Resources are going to be deployed to reinforce strong and motivating brand associations in the future brand strategy and perhaps to correct, diminish, or replace a misperception. Leaders should want the data so they will know where those resources should be used. What leaders don't know *can* hurt the institution in terms of wasted time and money, so allow the hard questions to be asked. There is often a way to structure a question so that it does not further emphasize or call attention to a problem. The research experts will be able to suggest a number of safe ways to ask.

Study Attributes and Qualities Specific to the Institution

Being too generic and testing claims that any institution can make are useless when it comes to building a strategy that differentiates it from competitors. Yes, the college excels at personal attention, and of course many students desire such attention, but most competitors can and do make the same claim. Sure, the university balances theoretical and classroom learning with practice and experiential learning. Those are table stakes that ensure that the institution has a place in prospective students' consideration, but they do not ensure that the institution will win them. Find the things that set the institution apart and ask about them, so you can determine whether those are authentic to the institution, relevant to the key audiences, and motivating to them so that they engage and act in ways that support the institution and build value. Related to this, think about the competition—what they represent and claim—and how the research can reveal true differentiators.

Use Multiple Research Methods

An institution just starting this process may be in a hurry and uninterested in taking the time to do both qualitative and quantitative research. Generally, one method improves the value of the other. Let the research experts help you determine the best methods according to the purpose, time, and money available.

Study the Stakeholder Audiences Who Most Influence Strategic Goals

Studying only prospective students and alumni gives a very limited sense of the brand. Some of the most important influences on the perceptions of the institution's brand are those who deliver on its promise (or don't) every day. Internal audiences, including faculty, staff, and students, can be studied in timely and effective ways. Their input and buy-in will be needed when it comes to building and expressing the brand strategy. It is always better to hear it at the beginning, when those perceptions can be accounted for, than when the institution's rollout of the brand expression is met with a clamor of resistance.

Similarly, it is dangerous to rely solely on internal audiences, whose views might not be objectively grounded in the reality of external audience perceptions. The goal of brand research is to develop a strategy that feels authentic to internal audiences and is relevant and motivating to external audiences whose awareness and support will be needed to build value—prospective students, their parents, alumni, donors, peer leaders at other institutions, and state legislators, for example. It is always better to study a mix of both internal and external audiences.

Anticipate Replication of the Research in the Future

Make sure that the areas of study and questions asked can be replicated in a few years to measure progress and make adjustments to the strategy in the future. The research experts can help ensure that this is addressed.

Market Research Beyond Brand Building and Refinement

Other kinds of market research than brand research may be useful to an institution. These kinds of research can be delivered by the same resources (internal or external) and generally serve more narrow or discrete purposes. Often, institutions with more mature and healthy brands have the time and resources to engage in these kinds of research. Some of the types used in higher education include pricing, market demand, customer acquisition, and segmentation studies.

Pricing

These studies seek to understand what the target audience views as the optimal price, in light of competitors' prices, for a program, service, or experience. Increasingly, institutions are studying *price elasticity*, or the change in demand based on a change in price. Institutions whose demand is subject to great variability, depending on the cost, are institutions with *elastic* demand. Institutions whose demand changes little or not at all when the price changes are said to have *inelastic* demand. Think of the most revered higher education brands: these have inelastic demand.

Institutions may hope that changing tuition rates (full list price) or net price (total cost after financial aid discount) might motivate more students to apply, or they fear that fewer will apply. A regional public university that sets its tuition rate one dollar higher than that of the state's flagship research university might hope to signal quality similar or equal to the flagship's. A college might consider a strategy of dramatically reducing both list price and discount rate to improve the perception of affordability and access. Before an institution proceeds to make a change, a pricing study can estimate the impact and even identify a sweet spot that combines ideal tuition and discount rate to yield maximum net tuition revenue, as Stamats did for American University a few years ago.

Market Demand

It is unwise to consider starting a new program based on academic and faculty interests alone, though many institutions do. It is reasonable for boards that are attuned to their fiduciary responsibilities to ask for evidence that a new degree program's costs can be sustained, if not initially then eventually, by enrollment prior to giving their approval. Ideally, market demand analysis should be built into the shared governance process for evaluating and proposing new programs, since they will require financial and human investments including, but not limited to, the educational costs. For example, what will be required to develop awareness and interest in a new program (web pages, collateral, advertising)? Does the market demand suggest a projected enrollment that will recoup those investments and generate net revenue?

Methods for estimating market demand include looking at "births" and "deaths" of programs that started or stopped producing graduates in a field of study with the same or similar degree name in the institution's competitive market for students. IPEDS is a source of information used to produce this analysis, and familiarity with the data set is important, so looking for a firm or internal expert that has that knowledge and experience is important. Another method for studying market demand is to explore the recent and current position postings of employers in the relevant markets to estimate potential future demand for degree requirements associated with positions in high demand. Organizations like the Education Advisory Board, Eduventures, and Burning Glass provide research on market demand for higher education institutions, and many local research firms may as well. Another good resource is Georgetown's Center on Education and the Workforce, which specializes in research, reports, and data focused on the link between education, career qualifications, and workforce demand. Finally, online program managers (OPMs), who provide recruitment services and delivery of online programs, use program demand estimates to determine the level of return on their investment. Even if the method is not shared by an institution's partner OPM, it may at least share whether it categorized potential programs as having high, medium, or low demand.

Customer Acquisition

Studies that seek to determine why customers do or do not choose a program or service fall into the category of customer acquisition. The Admitted Student Questionnaire is a College Board product used by many admissions offices that use College Board services.

Segmentation

Institutions with mature marketing practices may wish to tailor aspects of the marketing mix to different segments of an audience. Messages (promotion), cost (price), program or service offering (product), or method of access or delivery (place) may be varied and focused by segment to yield stronger results. For example, segmenting alumni audiences to understand what motivates them to join, give, or participate can improve the cost-effectiveness of annual fund campaigns, membership drives, marketing for attendance at events, or targeting for philanthropic campaigns.

A Clear Roadmap for the Work Ahead

Market research is the first step in laying the foundation for development of a brand strategy and should be the basis of any adjustment of an existing brand strategy. It will serve as the roadmap, discipline, and insurance policy for the strategy over the long term. It is useful for leaders to be aware of and mindful of their roles and responsibilities in the process since they will invest in and use the results of the research to form strategy, and they should also value the roles that others in the community play in this process. The role of research experts with experience and appreciation for higher education is particularly important.

A research process tied to the institution's strategic goals helps it determine the purpose, methods, cost, and time to complete the brand research. The process ensures that the research questions and results are carefully formed and vetted at key points to build buy-in and support for the conclusions and implications for the decisions about brand strategy (the focus of the next chapter). Other forms of market research with more discrete and narrow purposes may be employed to address a particular issue, opportunity, or concern.

Key Questions for Leaders and Their CMOs

- Do we know how our brand is perceived by key stakeholders (especially those outside the institution)? Is our knowledge based on data or anecdotes?

- Are we willing to commit time and resources to meaningful market research that will inform strategic decision-making?

- What are the primary goals of our market research strategy? What do we need to know in order to make the best decisions?

Chapter 4

What's the Big Idea?

Developing Brand Strategy and Expression

It was important to have an inclusive and grassroots process, to get input from internal constituencies. Showing faculty, staff, and students the research results fostered buy-in.
> —Karl Einolf, president, Indiana Tech

Building on the premise that intelligence from key stakeholders about the institution and its competitors will be the foundation for a strategy that serves as a roadmap to building value and is built to last, this chapter focuses on the process of developing or refining a brand strategy and the means to express it through a series of creative tools and institutional decisions. The process for developing, expressing, and refining an institutional brand is described, and then the issues of roles and responsibilities, capacity and expertise, resource requirements, and mistakes to avoid are presented.

The Process of Developing a Brand Strategy

Building or refining a brand requires identification of a series of foundational elements and insights emerging from market research to develop a platform on which decisions about institutional positioning and communication will rest. Essential tools

for building this platform include (1) a series of design requirements that will serve as the basis for shaping and evaluating the
developing strategy and its expression and (2) a rubric to guide
the construction.

Design Requirements

Recall that in chapter 1 we reviewed perspectives on characteristics of a strong brand. Higher education marketing and branding experts may use slightly different language to describe the
basic elements of effective brands, but their approaches share
some elements in common. Susannah Baker and Anna Meyers
advocate a simple framework of three requirements: real (authentic and true), rare (differentiating among competitors), and
relevant (meaningful to stakeholders).[1] To build the brand platform and its expression at both the University of Maryland and
American University, I relied strongly on a set of four design requirements, similar to Baker and Meyers's three Rs but adding
the requirement of simplicity (table 2). This addition adds a degree of difficulty that is challenging but critical.

In order for a brand strategy to work, decisions must be made
about what will be prioritized or elevated. If not made deliber-
ately, the decisions will inevitably be determined by the limits
of resources, time, and memory, and often unintentionally. Practically, decisions to strengthen the institution's position are necessarily limited by resources. Similarly, a small number of institutional priorities are at the root of experiences that faculty and
staff create every day, as they interact with students, alumni,
donors, community and business leaders, and citizens, among
others, essentially delivering on the brand promise. And finally,
brand expression aims to establish a few main brand associations with the college or university, because audiences can't and
won't recognize, remember, and recall too many. Leaders who
steward strong brands make these choices about priorities delib-
erately so that the brand strategy is intentionally reinforced.

TABLE 2. *Design requirements for effective brands*

- **R**elevant: Meaningful and motivating to a broad range of stakeholders
- **A**uthentic: Accurately representative of where the institution is and where it is headed
- **D**ifferentiating: Distinguishes the institution from direct competitors
- **S**imple: Easy to grasp, remember, and recall

It's not in the nature or culture of academics to elevate a few strong choices. Here again, the inclination to be comprehensive and detailed in describing all aspects of the institution should be resisted. Practical limits allow only a few ideas to come through and be memorable and should warrant courageous action. Be intentional about what to elevate. "This idea of marketing a certain field and not just everybody—that was really important," says Troy Hammond, of North Central College. He emphasizes that it was only possible through a huge effort to educate the community, keeping faculty, staff, and the board informed and involved throughout a grassroots-oriented process. "It was clear that we were going to pick an area or two where we are really excellent. At some point, we had to put a stake in the ground." When asked how that was received by the community, Hammond shared the feedback from an influential faculty member, who told him, "I'm fine if that means more students at North Central."[2]

One way to keep the strategy simple is to limit the number of key associations or messages being reinforced, whether about programs, character, or personality. At the University of Maryland, market research and mission led us to focus on four key pillars of the original brand strategy: discovery, quality, impact, and momentum. The first three helped distinguish Maryland's mission—as a research university, a land-grant institution, and the flagship of the University System of Maryland—from the missions of all the other public universities in the system and the state. Discovery, used to describe the university's research mission, resonated particularly with business leaders, voters, and state elected leaders as a valued and noble role for a university to play, in addition to producing graduates and serving the state. Momentum helped distinguish the university from other research institutions with similar missions. The rapid rise in its student and faculty quality, scholarship, fundraising, and other measures of performance hastened the university's arrival among top research institutions, changing its market position in a short period of time. This trajectory conveyed a powerful sense of energy and progress that was noticeable to stakeholders and competitors alike. A vice-president of corporate communication for a major telecommunications firm observed approvingly, "You're telling other top research universities, Maryland has the same level of quality and impact that you do, but we got here faster than the rest of you. Move over, and watch out, we just might pass you." The four key pillars, along with elements of mission and personality, were expressed through two brand campaigns, first "ZOOM" and then the successful and long-lasting "Fear the Turtle." Elements of this platform remain two decades later in the current brand expression, "Fearless Ideas." Both the small number of elements in the strategy and the short, memorable expressions are simple, in addition to being relevant, authentic, and differentiating.

At American University, the original brand strategy had three primary brand pillars: active citizenship, learning from leaders, and Washington as a powerful lab for learning. Granted, they were a little more wordy, but they represented a small number of items that emerged from the institution's founding as a national university to train "public servants for the future," along with elements of its statement of common purpose, emphasizing its historical strengths in public policy and public affairs, international relations, and law, or "public service, writ large,"[3] and strengths that were evident in market research (regarding the quality of faculty, the frequent visits of world leaders to campus, and the abundance of internships, experiential learning, and research opportunities in the nation's capital). Along with some elements of personality and character, the platform provided the basis for the "WONK" campaign. *Wonk*—the word *know* spelled backwards—was a term often associated with policy and experts in other fields and disciplines who were passionate about their subject and used their knowledge to create meaningful change.

Certainly a one-word phrase to describe a whole institution was a tall order, but it was flexible enough to represent all kinds of students and faculty who were smart, passionate, engaged, and focused on using their knowledge to create meaningful change. Short and memorable, it made AU's first brand campaign stand out (differentiating) from those of universities in Washington with similar programs and missions and older, more established reputations. Also highly relevant and authentic, it was the basis for nearly a decade of success in building a stronger brand that was evident in dramatic increases in first-year applications and yield rates, a higher percentage of students for whom AU was first choice, increased alumni engagement, and higher rankings.

Leaders will find variations on the theme of these design requirements for strong brands when they work with partner agencies, but the core themes remain. When working with a partner, ask to see their approach and choose one that appeals and is suitable to the institution's culture and context.

Bill Faust, at Ologie, says that his agency relies on a framework of five design requirements: unique, authentic, relevant, sustainable, and motivational. Faust concedes that uniqueness is difficult to achieve among higher education brands. "Higher education wasn't designed to be unique, but be unique within your market," in the context of head-to-head competitors. He notes that either the strategy or the expression (or both) should be highly differentiating or rare. To borrow from an example in the automotive sector, Volvos and BMWs are both cars in a class of luxury, high quality, and cost, but Volvo differentiates on safety, boldly pledging in 2016 to eliminate deaths and serious injuries from car accidents by in the year 2020.[4] BMW differentiates on performance, referring to its cars as the "Ultimate Driving Machine."

Faust also rightly emphasizes the need for sustainability. For brands to work, they need to last, usually a lot longer than the point at which internal stakeholders are reaching fatigue and hankering for something new. Finding a strategy that is flexible and sustainable enough to last in the context of the normal evolution of the institution, including changes in programs or leadership, is a smart play. Dan Mote, president at the University of Maryland when we shaped the original brand strategy, liked to say it should "have legs." He wanted us to choose a focus that had the potential to last a long time. "Fear the Turtle" and its underlying strategy definitely had legs.

Elizabeth Johnson emphasizes that the relevance of criteria varies for stakeholders. In figure 2, she demonstrates that the platform on which the ideal brand strategy rests lies at the intersection of concise strengths that matter to all of the stakeholders and that differentiate the institution from competitors. For internal audiences, the strategy must be authentic and valued. For external audiences, it must be desired (motivating) and matter (relevant). Finally, any strategy chosen must be distinctive and compelling relative to those of competitors, in that it isn't credibly claimed or owned by others in the institution's primary market.

In this roundup, it is clear that experts share a view that the design requirements for a brand strategy must include differentiation, authenticity, and relevance. I hold out for ideas in strategy and expression that are simple, because they help with internal adoption and external recognition and recall early in the process. Good counsel from marketing leaders should be applied to the institutional context, and they should help leaders use what fits best.

Rubric for the Brand Platform

The second tool in the toolbox for building and expressing a brand strategy is a rubric that defines the strategy elements and

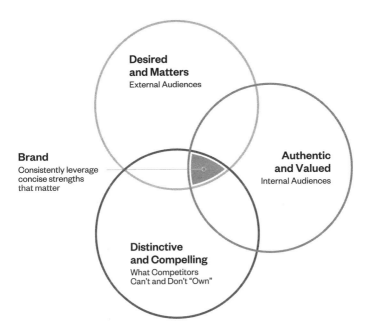

Figure 2. Brand platform. Brand strategy should leverage strengths that matter to internal and external audiences and that differentiate the institution from competitors. Courtesy of SimpsonScarborough.

their relationship to one another. This is the blueprint for building the brand structure. It will literally serve as the foundation for decisions about brand expression and institutional investments that will deliver and reinforce the strategy over time. While the final brand platform document may include lots of other information as context (rationale for the brand or rebrand initiative, timing, relationship to institutional strategy, process and participants, key research takeaways, and next steps), a one-page, high-level summary of the elements is the key deliverable, and it is a powerful map to guide the institution in this work.

Rob Moore, vice-president for communication and marketing at CASE, one of the largest global education associations in the world, is also CEO emeritus of Lipman Hearne. Rob literally wrote the book on building higher education brands—*The Real U: Building Brands That Resonate with Students, Faculty, Staff, and Donors*—which I commend to CMOs and other interested leaders. The book describes the process in detail and provides dozens of great examples. Moore advocates a simple rubric developed by his company that stands the test of time and is an easy one to describe.[5] (Other firms will have similar tools with many of the same elements, perhaps illustrated differently, but all working toward the same objective.)

In this rubric (fig. 3), six of the seven elements build on one another. From bottom to top they are:

- Mission
- Positioning
- Proof
- Pledge
- Personality
- Payoff

The seventh element, located right in the middle, near the top, is called the Big Idea. This is the brand essence, what Moore calls "a short-hand answer to the question, What is this brand all about?"[6] Eventually, this will be the concept that is illustrated with storytelling, copywriting, design, photography, and video to fully convey the aspects of the brand platform. Moore points out that the mission is fundamental, the positioning and proofs are functional, the Big Idea and pledge are strategic, and the personality and payoffs are emotional—it is the emotional elements that really bring a brand to life and help it resonate with audiences.[7]

Whether using this or another template or rubric, the CMO or partner firm will help the institution work through its historical context (its past), the strategic plan's foundational elements (its present and future), any previous brand strategy or expression, and the market research findings (insights from stake-

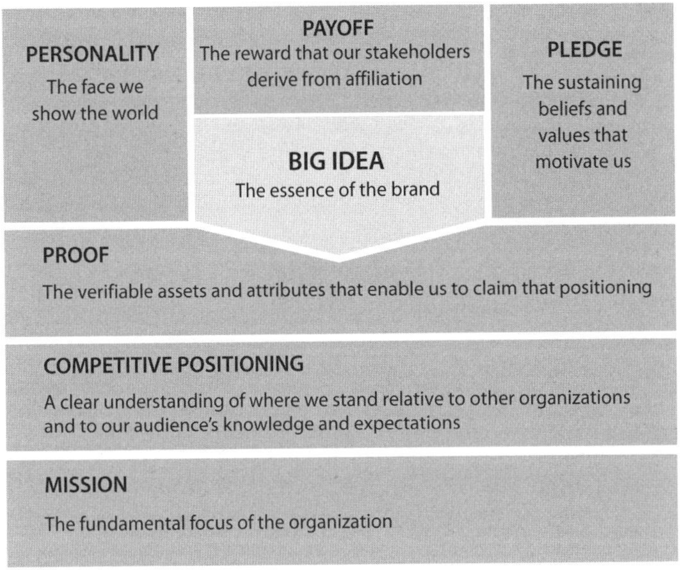

Figure 3. Sample brand template, illustrating key elements of the brand strategy. Courtesy of Lipman Hearne, Inc.

holders about the institution and its competitors). Often this involves conducting a series of exercises or activities with the marketing task force or equivalent that yield a developing brand platform.

A process of vetting the elements of the brand platform with representatives of various constituencies helps to refine the elements, and along the way it creates buy-in. Hammond at North Central College says the process of educating and involving the community and board included presenting and updating at faculty meetings and at all-staff meetings, as well as a significant investment of time by the board. "The board was involved from the very beginning, with an active discussion that I led. They were very engaged and set aside time at every meeting, and this ensured their buy-in. We were able to engage their expertise, and they learned some things. There are some great advocates on the board."[8]

Johnson likens the first draft of this positioning document to a fitting for a suit or a wedding gown. "It never fits the first time. You always have to vet the positioning a second and maybe even a third time to make sure it truly captures the essence of the institution. It's a little bit like tailoring."[9]

Leaders are advised to be patient at this stage. Faster is not better. Taking the time to get things right at this point in the process will save time and money and avoid heartache later. I'm reminded of a point when most members of the marketing task force at American University were satisfied with the brand platform, with the exception of the provost, an important participant, who held out for more. He felt that the institution's ambitious plans for scholarship with greater impact and a student experience with greater rigor, both prominent in the strategic plan, were not evident in the positioning. It was clear that a step back was needed to get him on board. If we didn't have his support, we wouldn't have the support of the president, the faculty, or the board. Johnson, our partner on research and strategy recalls, "That suit did not fit the provost the first time we presented it. It was just a little bit off—the sleeves were too long, or something. He said he just didn't feel like it represented the ambitious future of the university. It was misaligned with these new bright-shining-star faculty they were bringing on board."[10]

I arranged a luncheon meeting for the president, the provost, Johnson, and me. The talk was candid. A lot about the work to date was well aligned, but the academic ambition in the strategic plan was not evident. Johnson realized that the recently hired faculty represented "what they were gunning to accomplish for the institution."[11] Despite our timeline and the deadlines for next steps, we agreed to stop and do some more interviews, specifically with 15 high-profile faculty scholars. That was huge for the president's confidence in our process, especially because of the respect it showed the provost.

We listened to why these faculty had come to American. We asked them to "try on" the draft positioning and see how it fit. Mostly, they supported and echoed what they saw, but they added some of their ambition for scholarship and academic rigor, expressed through the positioning that had already been developed. Their input improved the draft. In the end, the provost came aboard, and the tailored positioning statement fit the institution like the custom-made outcome it needed to be.

The design requirements are incredibly helpful in evaluating the fit. They can be used as a filter, to evaluate how well the draft is working toward developing a strategy that is authentic, relevant, differentiating, and capable of being sustained over the long term. (Bonus points if the strategy elements are free of academic jargon and if the big idea is easy to state and recall.)

The market research can also be an excellent touchstone to come back to. At American, we tested a series of possible positioning statements in our stakeholder surveys, which had emerged from 90 preliminary interviews. Elements of three of these statements appealed strongly to prospective students as attractive in a college, were considered authentic and accurate by internal audiences, and were appealing to alumni as a direction for the future of the institution. Convergence among these important stakeholder groups helped us focus on the elements of positioning that would form a critical part of our brand platform. Descriptions of the university community as politically active, passionate, engaged, broad-minded, global, and focused on meaningful change gave us personality to convey in the platform.

At Maryland in the late 1990s, the lack of awareness among most audiences of the distinct mission and value of a research university, as compared with other public institutions, put differentiation as a research institution front and center in the strategy. The research also showed us that most Maryland voters and state legislators found the terms *research* and *scholarship* a bit aloof and thought they detracted from the goal of educating students, which they saw as our primary mission. However, *discovery* sounded appealing and inspirational, and the application of discoveries to benefit society and local communities was a direct benefit they could relate to and appreciate. Aspects of the university character and personality, such as being fiercely determined and always moving forward, as well as often being underestimated yet often outperforming competitors, were also part of the brand platform. This led in the creative expression to the confident—not arrogant—and slightly tongue-in-cheek attitude of "Fear the Turtle," which also harkened back to the parable of the tortoise and the hare. The key findings of the research should always be addressed in the brand platform so that the creative team will benefit from that guidance and intelligence.

The culmination of the strategy process is a significant milestone, but it is really only the halfway point. The development of the brand platform serves two primary purposes, according to Bill Faust at Ologie: "It creates internal alignment, and it provides inspiration to the creative team."[12] The culmination of the internal alignment comes from informing the leadership and obtaining their support for the basic brand platform as a strategy document. Only then can it be handed off to the creative team to guide the brand expression.

However, passing this milestone can also be challenging in that the strategy is not the expression itself. It won't be published anywhere publicly, and it won't be found on a website or in a brochure or digital ad. Sometimes it is frustrating for academic leaders and boards to support the strategy conceptually because they can't imagine its use until they see examples of creative expression. Bill Faust likes to remind leaders that "the brand strategy is the brand promise, and the story of that promise is the brand expression."[13] No matter how much they want to see the brand expressed, it is important at this stage to obtain support for the concepts or ideas in the strategy. Once that is achieved, it is on to the creative development.

Brand Expression

At last, with the strategy completed, the work of the creative team begins. Whether that is an internal team or an outside firm, the balance of art and science in this process tilts slightly more to art, informed by the data and the strategy. With a background that leans more toward data and strategy, I'm almost in awe of the magic that happens in this part of the process. I've only caught glimpses, because I firmly believe that it's the job of leadership to set the team up for success and then step back. Setting them up for success means giving them time and creating an environment in which an explosion of ideas can be generated by an excellent briefing and then they have the freedom to explore, ideate, and iterate.

Creative Teams: Internal or External

Several times I have relied on an internal team to come up with the big idea. At American, I provided the team with space that was open, light, comfortable, and conducive to creativity. (Picture palm trees, full-size Elvis cutouts, Christmas lights, beanbag chairs, Play-Doh, crayons, markers, Post-it notes, and newsprint taking over a conference room, with all the usual furniture moved out, for a month.) We called it the "war room" because of the intensity and chaos that characterize parts of the process—there is a good bit of "storming" in brainstorming.

As important as space is time. This process takes time to yield quality. Creative professionals follow a process and discipline that is as important as that of an architect or engineer. It also requires focus. With my internal teams, we arranged for those participating in the creative process to clear the decks of their normal work. This means that other members of the team play just as important a role, picking up the slack of additional work for a number of weeks. Alternatively, other projects and priorities can be delayed or staged to follow this period of intense focus.

Members of an internal creative team should be led by the CMO or someone designated by the CMO. This should be a seasoned marketing professional who has had experience using strategy to guide creative work. I've benefitted from having senior team members with agency and broadcast marketing experience; they were like orchestra conductors leading highly accomplished musicians. These senior team members knew when to press and when to lay back and let the expertise run, when to bring the group back to strategy and requirements, and how to keep them on track in terms of timing and deliverables.

The team's membership should be interdisciplinary. Staff with experience in advertising, newswriting, copywriting, editing, design, photography, videography, media relations, digital, user experience, and social media, with their range of training and perspectives, will address the task better than a team of designers would on their own. If the team includes staff who are alumni or long-time employees, it will be important for the team leader to watch for and identify any blind spots or absence of objectivity they may have because of their closeness to the context of the work.

If internal teams have the advantage of familiarity and the limit of lack of objectivity, an outside firm has the advantage of objectivity and the limit of lack of familiarity. If working with an outside firm, the leadership should expect the account lead at the agency and the CMO to complete a strong handoff of the strategy and research to the creative director and team for the next phase of the process, with occasional check-ins and minimal interference until they are ready to share some alternatives.

According to Faust, "This is the time to brief the creative team on the strategy and get out of their way for a while."[14] This will require a high-level understanding of the key takeaways of the market research, familiarization with the context of audiences and competitors, and a deep dive on the brand platform. Some firms or teams will use a creative brief, a tool used by agencies to crisply articulate strategy and requirements to frame the work ahead. This is an internal document that won't see the light of day elsewhere; it is only used to inform and inspire the creative team.

Whether internal or outsourced, the creative team must immerse themselves in the strategy that preceded their work. Allow them the time to absorb the strategy and then start with the widest possible lens. They may want to look at what all the other competitors are saying and doing, for example, so that the expression, as well as the strategy, is differentiating. Then the brainstorming begins, somewhat unrestrained but ultimately tethered to the strategy and design requirements. Faust says his team uses a process called "Shallow and Wide." The interdisciplinary team begins by generating dozens of divergent ideas and then slowly begins to narrow. A process of funneling and convergence, after wide ideation, ensures that the team doesn't squelch any good ideas. Similar ideas may merge, and the team starts to focus more closely on a few promising directions.[15]

Ultimately, the creative team should aim for two different concepts that both effectively address the strategy. The team will spend some time developing "spec work," or enough creative execution to present the two concepts in compelling ways. The presentation of these concepts shouldn't be fully polished— there will be plenty more to do once a concept has been chosen— but developed enough that those who need to see the concepts described and illustrated can begin to imagine the possibilities.

Choosing the Concept

The team, and eventually the CMO, the marketing task force, and the leadership, should continue to be guided by the design requirements of authenticity, relevance, and differentiation, along with sustainability and simplicity. These requirements act as a filter, along with the brand platform, for evaluating the strengths and weaknesses of the two concepts. They also establish parameters that avoid defaulting to personal taste in color, design, or writing style.

Returning to the example of "WONK" at American, we presented two concepts to the marketing task force for their consideration and recommendation. Each member of the task force had the one-page summary of the brand platform in front of them, and we reminded them of the design requirements for a strong brand. One concept was a traditional, handsome-looking presentation that played off the name American, and it would have made Ralph Lauren very proud. The other was the concept of KNOW/WONK, with a modern design, a bold and confident attitude, and a story to tell of AU people devoted to using their passion to achieve meaningful change (fig. 4). Both would have served the university well and the creative team was prepared to execute on either choice.

I told the task force members that I did not want them to vote. I wanted a consensus recommendation to the cabinet after we

Figure 4. Sample display ad from American University's "KNOW/WONK" campaign. Courtesy of American University.

discussed the strengths and weaknesses of each concept. I started with the handsome American option and asked for strengths. Every response kept referring back to a contrast that explicitly favored WONK. After trying to keep the focus on the first concept, I pivoted to WONK, and the energy in the room rose palpably. There were strengths and weaknesses in relation to the brand platform, to be sure. But it was clear that one concept overwhelmingly addressed the strategy more effectively and met the requirements for a strong brand better than the other. Finally, I asked for a recommendation. Wholeheartedly, the group went for WONK. A few had reservations (related to issues we saw in the creative testing, as noted in the next section) but felt they could support the recommendation. The president's chief of staff asked for a show of hands for each concept to convey the strength of the recommendation. It was a landslide for WONK.

After the task force overwhelmingly recommended the concept of KNOW/WONK to the leadership, the cabinet considered the concept in light of the brand platform and the design requirements, reviewing the task force's feedback. The concept was authentic and real. It conveyed messages that were relevant and motivating to a range of stakeholder audiences. It was so differentiating that most felt there was no way our competitors would ever embrace such a bold approach. It was certainly simple and memorable, it was flexible enough to be used for a range of different parts of the university, and we could imagine it being sustained for some time. The cabinet approved the recommendation on the conditions that no deal-breaking risks surfaced in creative testing and that the concept's expression would be refined based on the results.

Creative Testing

The value of putting the concept or concepts in front of target audiences cannot be understated. Focus groups react and describe what is coming across, how it makes them feel, and what they might be motivated to do as a result. Testing at this stage identifies risks, surfaces unintended and potentially embarrassing associations and responses, and provides ideas about how to improve the presentation of the concept to make it more appealing. Testing with representatives of different stakeholder audiences helps the institution understand which presentations of concepts speak most compellingly to all of them. This creative testing can occur after the preferred concept is chosen, to hone and refine it, or to inform decisions about the value of two alternatives. It can also be used to evaluate a current brand expression, to determine how it should be refined or evolved.

An opportunity exists to record or observe the testing in person. Johnson says she wishes she could get every president she works with behind a one-way glass in a focus group facility to watch the reactions. Nothing substitutes for watching the nonverbals and hearing the voices of stakeholders engage with or dismiss a concept. That may not be possible or realistic, but as CMO I observed every focus group's reaction to WONK, and those observations virtually unlocked the secrets to the campaign's success. When presented with a black presentation board with WONK in simple white lettering, most prospective and current students inevitably sat back with quizzical looks and said that the word was unfamiliar and sounded funny. But when they were shown the origin of the word (*know* spelled backwards) and were given a definition of a wonk as a passionate expert who uses their knowledge to create meaningful change, their expressions changed to smiles, they sat forward in their chairs, and they described how "cool" and "clever" (my words, not theirs) they thought it was.

Faculty, staff, and alumni had some familiarity with the word *wonk*, but the association was dated and not always positive. *Nerdy* was mentioned more than once, and associations were limited to policy experts. However, when we showed them examples of people who referred to themselves proudly as wonks of all sorts in news accounts, they were willing to consider an updated definition. When we showed them examples of confident, proud, passionate experts of all sorts—science wonks serious about climate change and legal wonks passionate about social justice—they were off and running, describing how AU could use the concept in lots of ways we hadn't even begun to imagine. One of the keys to the success of "WONK" was leaning into KNOW as the origin of the word, a good starting place for a university's brand, and the way to introduce and define the concept. Another was proving through creative presentations that AU's passionate students, faculty, staff, and alumni fit a more updated definition of the word, coming into more frequent use in the press just as we were getting ready to claim it. Without this intelligence, we surely would have run right into those reactions without properly accounting for them and adjusting the creative expression.

Vetting the Strategy and Concept

Sharing the creative expression of the brand with stakeholders before launch is a critical aspect of the branding process. In the age of social media, introducing the brand to your community at launch is like one roommate inviting another to a party in the home they share. It will not go well, and the resentment will be lasting and perhaps disabling. Of course, it is difficult to share the strategy and execution with every student, faculty, staff member, and alumnus before launch, but if the process has been open and participatory at key milestones and a reasonable effort has been made to get the input and guidance of constituency leaders along the way, then the debut of the brand launch won't be a shock and is more likely to be a cause for celebration of shared work than an opportunity to tear it down.

Karl Einolf, at Indiana Tech, sees the importance of the president serving as a champion of an inclusive process, underlining its strategic importance and regularly communicating about it.

It was important to have an inclusive and grassroots process. That was important to get input from internal constituencies. The research with internal audiences helped us with that. Showing faculty, staff, and students the results fostered buy-in. Now my job is to remind everyone that we have a strategic plan and we are moving forward to execute it. You have to keep communicating and repeating it. Every time I speak, I talk about the goals in the strategic plan. Some are still hearing it for the first time, even though we repeat it over and over again. The repetition is critical.[16]

At American, we regularly communicated about the process of developing a brand. In addition to campus-wide letters from me as CMO and campus town halls hosted by the marketing task force, we invited all faculty, staff, students, and alumni to participate in the stakeholder study and explicitly shared the purpose of the research. When the brand platform was recommended and approved, we shared it with the entire internal community and posted it in our internal portal as a document that was password-protected and read-only. I made presentations to the leadership of internal constituency groups at the beginning of the process, as well as after we completed the market research and again when we completed the brand platform. The president updated the entire community on our progress in his periodic letters to the campus community.

At the point when we had a recommended concept for the brand's expression, I turned to retail politics. I hosted 35 luncheons and teas of 12 participants each, mostly faculty but also staff and student leaders. The groups were small enough to allow for individual participation, and not so large that they could overwhelm me in opposition. Over the course of a meal, I presented the strategic rationale for engaging in branding, the key takeaways from the research, and the brand platform and then introduced the concept of WONK, starting with KNOW. The approach had been modified following creative testing, and the creative presentation had matured to the point that it was becoming more polished, but not quite finished.

At each event, rather than asking for participants' approval or preference I asked, "What might you suggest to make this approach stronger? How would you see yourself using this concept? How do we engage other faculty, staff, and students in making it something we all can be proud of?" At the end of each session, we discussed next steps and timing so that participants were in the know and knew what to expect.

Over the course of this vetting process I gained ten pounds (no one eats lunch sandwiches and tea cakes every day for a month or more and escapes without impact), yet there were also far more desirable gains. We increased internal awareness of the brand initiative, developed greater buy-in prior to launch, identified dozens of good ideas for how to build out the brand expression and make it better, and identified both advocates and critics. We were able to build the advocates into our plans for launch; as for the critics, if we didn't persuade them, at least we had a better sense of their concerns and were prepared to address them.

Launch

There are differing approaches to implementing the brand strategy. Some institutions and agencies prefer to quietly begin using it in search materials, websites, alumni messages, and a host of other integrated marketing communications without fanfare. They integrate and build the presence of the brand strategy incrementally. Others prefer to introduce it intentionally, with recognition and fanfare that a new era is at hand. The former approach usually occurs without notice, for good or for ill. The latter might attract attention and become a lightning rod for resistance to change. I urge leaders to think of the investment of time and resources in this strategic initiative. When a building is opened, after months of planning and significant resources invested in the design and construction, certainly there is fanfare to mark the occasion. From the groundbreaking and topping-off ceremony to the ribbon cutting at the opening, there are rituals to reinforce the significance of the project and its intended impact. It would seem to me that claiming milestones and infusing them with meaning that relates to the strategic purpose is as appropriate for the branding initiative as it is for any other significant investment in the institution's future. Doing it in a way that emphasizes the benefits that will accrue to the institution would be important. The CMO and creative team or agency, who know or have come to know the institution in the course of their work, may have the best ideas about how to launch the brand.

Roles and Responsibilities

The responsibilities in the development of the brand platform and expression are very similar to those at the research stage. The president is an important champion whose support puts the work in a strategic context. The president's demonstrated support throughout the process reinforces the relevance for internal audiences, especially in the early going. The president and the cabinet are the decision-makers; they receive the recommendations about strategy and expression from the campus-based marketing task force of constituency representatives and subject matter experts. The CMO is the conductor of the entire process, working first with the research experts or outside agency in concert with the marketing task force to develop the strategy and then with the creative team or agency and the marketing task force to develop the concept for the brand's expression. The board offers insight, expertise, and advocacy. The board's involvement from the beginning will result in buy-in and support that will be critical when it comes time to invest in support to develop and implement the strategy.

Brand Refinement

Throughout this chapter, we have identified ways that the branding process can apply to colleges and universities, whether they are starting from scratch or looking to update or refine their brand strategy and expression, whether they are working with agencies or taking the work in-house. Emphasis should be placed on the notion that the strategy should be long-lasting. Perceptions of a brand take time to establish or to change. Just to get the brand expression into integrated communication for enrollment, alumni engagement, and fundraising could take several cycles or academic years. That's why sustainability is one of the important design requirements to consider. The brand strategy should last at least as long as the institutional strategy and ideally until as far in the future as one can imagine. It is the roadmap that the institution should keep coming back to as it considers how to engage with stakeholders to build value.

In chapter 7, on measurement, the principle of periodic research to measure progress is emphasized. For an institution considering a shift in brand strategy, one important consideration should be what progress has been made and whether that indicates a need for shift in strategy. In addition, if there has been a plan for major change that reflects the potential for a different institutional position in the market, or if there has been a major crisis that might precipitate the need to address the harm in the strategy, research should provide the data-driven reasons for a shift. I would strongly caution that new leadership alone is not a reason to change the brand strategy. Frequent changes in the underlying strategy are expensive and confusing to the target audiences, who can't keep up with or don't believe them. Football and basketball coaches are known for their tendencies to dramatically change the team uniform when new leadership arrives just because they want to signal a new era. Presidents should know better.

However, changes in brand expression do happen more frequently, even when the underlying brand platform remains constant. Think of all the ways that Coca-Cola has expressed happiness over the years. Consider all the ways that Apple has conveyed that their intuitive designs enhance experiences and unleash imagination and creativity. How many ways has Nike encouraged amateur athletes to strap on the gear that professional athletes use and Just Do It? There are any number of ways to express a particular strategy, and if one concept has done its job as demonstrated in the research but is getting a little long in the tooth, or if it is not working and a fresh approach would be better, the investment may be worth it. But the time and money it takes to develop and implement a new expression should make leaders pause and consider whether the reasons for the update are compelling. Obviously, institutions who have adopted a new brand strategy are the most likely to change their creative expression.

For an institution considering a refresh, the process remains the same, with two additions. The original strategy and any research that has measured its effectiveness should be considered inputs at the outset of the new effort. The question of brand equity in the current expression should be explored. Is it recognized and recalled by audiences? Do they favor it strongly and positively? If not, a change might be warranted. In the case of obvious affinity and equity, proceed with caution in making any significant change. Johnson points to the example of Meredith College, the largest women's college in the country. Their brand was expressed with a campaign called "Going Strong," developed seven years ago with the support of Mindpower, a marketing firm that works with many higher education institutions. When SimpsonScarborough went in to do the research prior to a brand refresh, the college community was tired of the campaign. But in a retest of a study developed prior to the campaign's expression, the data from stakeholders pointed overwhelmingly to keeping the current campaign theme rather than turning to something new. "We told them they were crazy to consider a change. We totally recommended staying with it."[17]

The University of Maryland faced a firestorm of vocal and unhappy alumni and students when they introduced the ironically named "Unstoppable Starts Here," an attempt to move from "Fear The Turtle" to a brand expression that was intended to be more aligned with academic excellence and deemphasized the athletic origins of the preceding campaign.[18] The strong negative reaction prompted the administration to clarify that there was no intention to replace "Fear the Turtle." They found ways to maintain it and shifted more gradually over time to "Fearless Ideas," and iconic graphic references to the terrapin's shell remain throughout the brand's expression. Leaders are advised that strong equity doesn't evaporate easily. Sixteen years after "Fear the Turtle" was first launched and five years after the shift to "Fearless Ideas," a staff editorial in the student newspaper argued that the "charming" and "tongue-in-cheek" "Fear the Turtle" was far better than the "self-serious" "Fearless Ideas."[19] There had better be solid, strategic reasons for revolution or evolution.

Lessons Learned and Mistakes to Avoid

This chapter illustrates the process of developing a brand strategy and its creative expression through the experiences of some of the field's most respected professionals, as well as through the experiences of several presidents who have successfully navigated the process with their institutions. I asked each of them to share key takeaways, lessons learned, and mistakes to avoid. Several themes emerged.

Plan Institutional and Brand Strategy Together and Let the Research Inform Both

"Ideally, institutional strategy informs brand strategy," says Faust. The data will inform both. "Putting data and rigor around the things we sensed and had perceptions about, made me confident and optimistic about the relevant metrics over time," says Hammond.[20]

Don't Rush It

"Faster is not better," says Johnson. Faust underscores the value that is being built over time. "It's playing the long game, like owning a home. If you take care of it, the equity will rise, or you can ignore it and the equity will erode," Hammond remarks. "There's a lot of intense pressure to do difference making. We have never viewed this as a short-term urgent change to try to combat those pressures; this is an investment in the long term. The institution will be in a better place five to ten years from now."[21]

Make the Process Inclusive

Part of the reason the process takes so much time is that the leadership needs to bring the community and key stakeholders along for the journey. Einolf emphasizes, "It was important to have an inclusive and grassroots process, to get input from internal constituencies. Showing faculty, staff, and students the research results fostered buy-in." Faust warns against a process that is too leadership driven or strictly top-down. "Alignment and collaboration are critical. People support what they help create. It's a fine line—it is not a democracy. I always say everyone gets a voice but not a vote. Let professional marketers use their expertise, but get as much input as you can and create as much collaborative space as you can. Because if it is a skunkworks thing and it's unveiled, it usually fails. People reject it, and it becomes totally subjective." Hammond found that the inclusion boosted the sense of community. "Engaging the whole community around the brand initiative is a positive, community building experience, not unlike the strategic planning process."[22]

Be the Champion

It's a fine balance. If stakeholders feel that the process has been top-down, they won't accept it. However, involvement and support by the CEO is essential. Hammond describes his involvement: "I had to be engaged in the scope and priorities, and I made sure I had a voice at the key milestones. I didn't steer or dictate though, especially on the creative side. We relied intensively on the research, and we engaged all the right constituents." Einolf advises, "You need the leadership of the institution to be in lockstep. If there is a planning task force, they have to be connected to the data, and that has to be connected to the team doing the market analysis and execution. If is just the CMO, it might be seen as 'just advertising.'"[23]

Don't Skip Past the Positioning and Brand Platform to Creative Expression

Moore cautions, "If you don't take the time to bring the campus community along with you, they won't get it. There is a strategic, deliberate element to be discussed with the community first, or they won't get where the creative came from."[24]

Don't Think of Brand Too Narrowly

"A brand is not a logo or tagline. It is much more holistic than that," says Faust.[25] All the work on research and strategy makes it clear that the process is much more than a pithy slogan.

Don't Change for the Sake of Change

If you have an existing strategy, Johnson warns, "don't come in with the mind-set that it all has to change. Our standard position is start where you are and continue what you are doing. How can we evolve this strategy that has been working for years now? How can we lean into or simply refine it to increase impact? If, as a leader, you just want to make your mark, you could totally be shooting yourself in the foot."[26]

Find the Right Partner

"This is not something we could have successfully undertaken with internal resources," says Hammond. "We have a great team, but this is not the kind of thing that would be easily or successfully undertaken with internal resources. For us it was clear and obvious. We needed a great partner that understands higher education and marketing in this day and age, the research and everything else. That's a huge key for us."[27]

Success and Impact

After such a huge investment of time, thought, and finances, it is reasonable to want to measure and demonstrate the impact a soon as possible. However, ultimately this process is about changing perceptions of an institution among stakeholders or reinforcing them in ways that inspire new levels of motivation, engagement and support. That doesn't happen quickly.

In the chapter on measurement the focus will be on midterm measures of behaviors that are aligned with brand support and long-term changes in perceptions that are measured through additional research. In the short term, however, it is wise to set up early indicators that the branding efforts have registered in a way that is more positive or neutral than negative. The CMO or agency will have ideas about how to register awareness and how to report and measure that in the early going.

In this day and age, social media will inevitably be part of the equation, but remember that social posts often reflect extremes, and more often than not they represent the complaint department. A plan to engage those who have not been along for the journey or don't understand how the institution arrived at the new brand expression should be in place before launch. Success is measured in terms of successfully addressing concerns while bolstering and reinforcing early support. Getting the new big idea over the hump in the early stages is a big part of the battle, and therein lies another reason to develop community buy-in before launch. With buy-in and a plan for launch, attention turns to integration of the big idea across the institution.

Key Questions for Leaders and Their CMOs

- Can we develop our brand strategy in parallel with our strategic planning process?

- Is our current brand platform relevant? authentic? differentiating? simple?

- What level of investment do we think it is necessary to execute on a new or refined brand platform? Are we prepared to support that level?

Chapter 5

Integration of the Brand across the Institution

Integration involves pursuing common goals in ways that combine and coordinate unit strengths and individual talents. It brings personal satisfaction, which by extension energizes your institution. But interaction also focuses and intensifies the potential for truly significant outcomes in times like these.
    —Larry Lauer, vice-chancellor emeritus, Texas Christian University

When an institution has developed a strategy that meets the requirements for a strong brand, with the input of stakeholders and leaders in an inclusive process, and launched it publicly through a creative expression, it is reasonable to feel a sense of completion. However, this is really a beginning, not an end. Granted, it is an important milestone, but the full value of such a process will only be realized when the strategy comes to life, in decisions about priorities that reinforce the institution's differentiated position among competitors and in the creation of experiences that live up to the promise of the strategy, as well as in marketing messages that repeat, repeat, and repeat the expression across all channels and among all key stakeholder audiences. A brand only builds value when it is leveraged at every opportunity, with harmony and redundancy that is evident in decisions, experiences, and communication. Integration of the strategy in decisions, service delivery, and marketing communication is an important next step.

Living the Brand: Don't Neglect the Other Three Ps

Recall from chapter 1 that the marketing includes a mix of four Ps: price, product, place, and promotion. Three of these four Ps have nothing to do with integrated marketing communication and everything to do with making decisions and creating experiences that reflect the institution's essence and reinforce a strategy that is differentiating, authentic, and relevant to target audiences. It is in price, product, and place that leaders have the greatest opportunity to reinforce and deliver on the brand strategy, although they can and should also influence the integrated marketing communication that tell the institution's brand story in communication for which they are responsible.

Price

Decision-making about what a stakeholder will pay, including all costs and all discounts, provides an opportunity to differentiate from competitors and reinforce desired associations in the brand strategy, particularly in terms of enrollment. List price for tuition, net price, tuition payment plans, and income share agreements are all forms of price that might be used to reinforce institutional brand strategy. For example, Simmons University and its online program manager, 2U, announced that starting in 2020 its graduate program in nursing would allow students to defer up to half their tuition until after graduation, interest free, and that payments would be capped at up to 10 percent of income.[1] The move is aligned with the institution's founding purpose—to educate and prepare women for lives of purpose, even before they had the right to vote—as well as its core values of investing in the community and preparing graduates for their life's work. Moreover, it reinforces recent initiatives to diversify and make the university more inclusive. This pricing strategy provided an opportunity to elevate brand awareness, build desired brand associations with the university, and increase consideration among prospective graduate students who otherwise would not be likely to consider the program's $67,000 price tag. The decision reflects differentiation, authenticity, and relevance.

Product

The decision to offer a new academic program, service, or activity—as well as the decision to stop offering ones that don't align with mission and strategy—can also reinforce the brand. An academic program that extends an institution's historical strength in one area with a new area of desired growth in an interdisciplinary program is one such decision. For example, a school with a strong public affairs program and recent growth in environmental science enrollment might offer and promote a new master's degree in environmental policy. An institution that wants to reinforce its commitment to student success might overhaul its core curriculum and first-year advising program with a goal to improve retention and smooth the transition for new students, as we did at American University.[2] An institution that wants to welcome more students from low-income backgrounds and support them in terms of improved graduate outcomes might seek to identify and fund transportation and other costs of participation in internship and study abroad programs, which already enjoy high participation rates for more privileged students. These are all examples of decisions about product that could reinforce an institution's brand strategy.

Place

Decisions that create access to programs and services for targeted markets can also reinforce brand position. Some of these decisions literally involve a new place, such as when Virginia Tech, located in Southwest Virginia, announced that it would build a new Innovation Campus in Northern Virginia, just outside Washington, DC, adjacent to Amazon's new second head-quarters, where it will offer graduate degrees in cybersecurity, artificial intelligence, and quantum computing, as well as a new incubator space.[3] The move allows Virginia Tech to enter the large and competitive market of adult learners and graduate de-gree seekers in Washington and provides opportunities for new partnerships with Amazon and other companies in these indus-tries, who already have a strong presence in the area and are hungry for qualified employees.

Similarly, Johns Hopkins University announced that it had purchased the building formerly occupied by the Newseum, lo-cated just blocks from the US Capitol.[4] With its primary campus and hospital located in Baltimore, Maryland, Hopkins for decades has had a presence in Washington, with four buildings around the city that housed, among other entities, its vaunted School of Advanced International Studies. The purchase of the new build-ing allowed consolidation of all the DC assets under one property with a visible premier address on Pennsylvania Avenue and rein-forced its strategy to expand its influence in public policy debates and increase enrollment in graduate policy programs.

Visitor centers for admitted students, alumni centers, resi-dence halls, and student unions are spaces that not only provide space for important institutional events and functions but also deliver experiences and create memories that strongly reinforce the brand. The Longaberger Alumni Center at Ohio State Uni-versity incorporates history, artwork, and artifacts that remind alumni of its mission and brand, while the lyrics of the school song rim the walls of a prominent lobby in the student union. The song's lyrics include the phrase *Time and change*, which is the name of OSU's strategic plan, and the theme for its sesquicentennial and its multi-billion-dollar fundraising campaign. According to Mi-chael Eicher, senior vice-president for advancement, "'Time and Change' has great meaning to our community. The words come from our school song, 'Carmen Ohio.' We sing it every time we get together. It is very powerful in this community and beyond."[5] Such repetition of meaningful brand associations in spaces, experiences, and communication represents powerful integration.

Some place decisions expand access virtually, not through a change in physical location. Decisions to offer online programs and hybrid executive programs that include remote learning and a few weekend intensive experiences onsite are examples of this kind of place decision. Philanthropy programs like planned giving provide a format or structure for more alumni to pledge significant gifts from their estates than would otherwise not be feasible. Alumni engagement through synchronous virtual participation in events is another example of variance of place in the marketing mix.

Any investment in priorities that reinforce strategy in tangible, noticeable ways helps to differentiate, build awareness, and eventually build engagement with and support for the brand. Leaders attuned to building value use annual decisions about strategic plan investments and budget priorities to align with the brand strategy. This is especially easy if the institutional strategy and the brand strategy have been developed in tandem or if one has meaningfully informed the other.

The Fourth P: Effective Promotion through Integrated Marketing Communication

Effective communication delivers and reinforces messages that develop awareness, engagement, and loyalty among key stakeholders of the institution, whose ongoing support is critical to building value. When the communication is integrated with the overall brand strategy and expression, it leverages the investment that has already been made, builds on that investment, and delivers greater value and effectiveness than if the communication stands alone.

According to Larry Lauer, "Integration involves pursuing common goals in ways that combine and coordinate unit strengths," and the interaction "focuses and intensifies the potential for truly significant outcomes in times like these"[6] when confronting the great challenges facing the higher ed sector. When stakeholders experience clear and unified reinforcement of the brand in many different contexts, the differentiated and relevant brand associations the institution wants to bring to mind are recognized and recalled more quickly, because repetition and frequency make them stick. This recall is the prerequisite for motivating behaviors that support the institution in meeting its primary goals.

Every department that uses resources for communication with a particular audience can leverage and benefit from the audience experiencing the same messages elsewhere. Think of it as a turbo boost for every single communication investment. Each investment enjoys the synergy of working from a platform that all are standing on and elevating. These include the following:

- Advancement
  - Philanthropic communication with donors and prospects to motivate gifts, including campaign branding as well as communication and media for campaign events
  - Alumni communication to motivate attendance, volunteer participation, and annual giving
- Athletics
  - Communication to season ticket holders and advertising sponsors to boost funding for athletic programs
- Community Relations
  - Communication with local neighbors and municipalities whose perceptions influence reputation and policy, whose support and engagement influence facilities planning and zoning, and whose interest in courses, arts, and cultural events generate revenue
- Enrollment
  - Marketing and communication to motivate undergraduate prospects to inquire, apply, and enroll

- Current student communication that promotes satisfaction, retention, and graduation
- Graduate marketing and communication to motivate prospective students to enroll in graduate programs
- Adult education marketing and communication to motivate application and enrollment in certificate, professional, and executive education programs
- Government Relations
  - Public communication to motivate engagement and advocacy in support of legislative positions that the institution favors
- Human Resources
  - Employment advertising and communication to recruit and hire faculty and staff
- Internal Communication
  - Communication representing key institutional initiatives to build awareness and support among faculty, staff, and current students
- Media and Public Relations
  - Communication with reporters, editors, and influencers to build awareness, support, and reputation
  - Crisis or issues management communication that seeks to address concerns and build support among stakeholders amid issues of controversy or alleged wrongdoing
- Parent and Family Relations
  - Communication to build supportive relationships that motivate advocacy and philanthropy
- Research and Scholarship
  - Marketing communication to build awareness, support, and reputation among peers and funding organizations

When investments and decisions about such communication are made independently, they represent inefficiency, waste, confusion, or lost opportunity. When they build on the brand strategy and expression, appropriate to each audience, they represent integration, efficiency and opportunity to build greater value.

Getting the power users, or "purveyors," of the brand, as Bill Faust calls them, to work together is no small feat. The decentralized responsibility for communication is spread throughout institutions, among staff who report to different leaders, often with their own primary goals and resources they independently control. As Lauer points out, the result is often that "marketing and communications veers off toward admissions. Fundraisers often use their budgets to hire outside experts in marketing and media. And because alumni relations has such a strong external focus, many alumni offices have enlisted outside technology and media consultants to help them expand their programs."[7] And that just accounts for the advancement professionals! At the largest institutions, this may mean hundreds of communicators interacting regularly with key stakeholder audiences, often with no coordination. At best, this results in lost opportunities to leverage the investments in branding for maximum impact. At worst, working in silos and at cross-purposes causes confusion and real harm.

Some of the greatest challenges to integration are in professional schools with established reputations and brands that precede work on an institutional brand strategy. Named business and law schools in particular and those operating on a responsibility-centered management (RCM) model, in which the academic unit is wholly responsible for managing its own revenues and expenditures, represent fertile ground for turf wars over brand marketing and communication alignment. Precedent often drives a separation that is neither necessary nor productive. Research can help to measure the academic unit's level of brand awareness and equity relative to those of the institution as a whole and whether key audiences recognize that the unit and the institution are connected. The aim of integration should be to build the brand equity in both the institution and the academic unit, and it is the responsibility of the CMO, the provost, and the dean or academic leader to make that happen, using the tools described in this chapter. The president may need to get involved to influence all concerned, to avoid the assumption that integration will harm the entity with the stronger brand equity. Brand equity is not a zero-sum game within an institution. More often than not, many things, well beyond aspects of the institution's logo and color, represent shared brand characteristics, and these can be the basis of integration.

I am not advocating for a corporate-style, centralized strategic communication function. Respect for academic freedom and autonomy for individual units and leaders have important history within our academic culture. However, that culture, with traditions of autonomy and decentralization, is lagging well behind other sectors that have already disrupted old practices and are setting new, heightened expectations for individualized, just-in-time service and personalized communication, anticipating customer needs through analytics and fully integrating the customer experience so that all parts of the company are aware of and contributing to the best possible experience.

When companies like Amazon, Uber, Airbnb, and the New York Times began using an integrated platform strategy to build their business model, they shaped expectations for the rest of us. A student who orders a product from Amazon in the morning is sitting in class or participating online later in the day, and she brings those expectations with her. It's not okay to bombard stakeholders with disjointed and uncoordinated outreach and communication. Leaders need to help prepare the people and culture of their institutions for the disruptions ahead, introduced by those expectations from other sectors. Deciding how to best represent the institution in terms of brand and associated marketing communication is a shared leadership responsibility that should be guided primarily by strategy and best practice, not individual turf or preferences.

Independent and autonomous power users of the brand can end up in siloed turf wars that inhibit an ultimate shared goal, which is to increase support for institutional goals through recognition and revenue. Leaders are in a position to head off such trouble and optimize the opportunities to build greater value by establishing a meaningful link between strategic initiatives and by encouraging communication that reinforces integration among them.

Tools to Promote Integration

A set of tools can facilitate greater integration for all of the units that play a role in conveying the brand to stakeholders. These are briefly described below to provide leaders with familiarity so that they will be equipped to set expectations that minimize conflict, enhance cooperation, and support the development and use of the tools by the CMO and others.

Leadership Modeling

The responsibility for coordinating integration of institutional marketing communication with the elements of the brand strategy is primarily the responsibility of the CMO, but conditions for encouraging and creating such integration are the responsibility of other executive leaders. As brand champion, the president must model such integration and set expectations for the rest of the team to do the same. The president should set the tone and expect any major strategic initiative or enterprise-level effort to be aligned closely with the brand strategy, and the CMO should be included as a strategic partner at the earliest stages. When the president provides vocal and demonstrated support for the importance of integrating the CMO into strategic initiatives, the CMO is more likely to be a critical and trusted partner for members of the leadership team, to understand the business goals of respective colleagues, and to more effectively integrate the brand strategy across the institution.[8]

The institution will have a head start if leaders have developed the strategic plan and brand strategy together through an inclusive process, informed by the same market research. Individuals feel a greater sense of ownership over something they helped to shape. For example, in my experience, if deans of business schools (often with marketing budgets far larger than I had at my disposal centrally) are involved in the development of the institution's brand strategy, they will be more likely to support alignment with the business school's marketing. In one instance, that meant waiting for the dean to see how the new university brand strategy and expression (which he helped to build) performed in the early going before he authorized his own marketing team to incorporate the concept in their business school marketing. In another, the dean was a marketing scholar and was inherently inclined to support alignment. It is great to have leaders on board from the start, but in the case of the more reticent academic partners, sometimes it is better to go with the willing and let the rest see that something is working before they hop on with support for integration and resources to implement it.

Brand Architecture

Another helpful tool is the articulation of brand architecture, which describes the relationship of parts of the institution using the brand. An excellent example is that used at North Carolina State University, which articulates the relationship of various parts of the organization based on mission and funding and uses this structure as the rationale for adherence to the brand expression and standards, as well as in circumstances that warrant more flexible use.[9] *Core brand* units serve the university's mission and receive funding, facilities, staffing, and material support from NC State. These include the academic colleges and schools and the advancement, admissions, and other units that adhere closely to the brand standards and platform. *Extended brands* also serve the NC State mission but receive their funding from NC State and outside groups. The Cooperative Extension Service and a research institute that receives partner funding fall into this category, and while expected to adhere to the brand standards and platform, they may also be given the flexibility to co-brand their organization to reflect joint support or affiliation. And finally, *sub-brands*, which receive support from both the university and outside groups, whose mission varies from the core university mission, including athletics and the alumni association, follow brand standards but are given flexibility to co-brand and use additional logos or trademarks. While this example focuses most heavily on the use of the logo or visual identity, it is a good example of how to base decisions about level of integration based on a rationale that is strategic, grounded in level of shared funding and purpose.

The resulting integration is evident in NC State's brand expression for the university, "Think and Do," and the brand expression in its fundraising campaign, "Think and Do the Extraordinary." Rarely is the integration so tightly linked in both design and strategy, and the results for both are powerful. Every campaign communication reinforces awareness of the overall brand strategy, while building on and leveraging the investments in it. (Additional tools for integration, such as NC State's brand tool kit, are publicly available on the university's website.)[10]

Use of the brand architecture gives leaders the ability to set expectations and avoid becoming mediators in conflicts between units, and it helps the CMO avoid being seen only as the "logo police," a role that diminishes the strategic nature of the CMO's position and responsibilities. This would be a particularly useful tool for laying out expectations for integration strategies between institutions and their most well-known academic units. The mission and the funding source for each school would be the basis for developing an appropriate level of integration or flexibility.

Audience Focus and Segmentation

Another device that helps to facilitate integration is segmentation. Segments are groups of people whose needs or desires are shared. Considering audiences as segments who share the same desire for certain benefits or seek to derive the same value from the institution puts the emphasis on communication that will be most effective with the audience rather than on which leader or department is primarily responsible for communicating with a particular audience. Departments or units that are responsible for delivering those benefits or values to a particular audience segment have a mutual responsibility and a shared interest in working with one another to communicate effectively. The CMO or agency partner can help the institution develop segmentation based on the market research and data that informed the brand strategy and facilitate efforts to coordinate the communication of units that target the same audiences or segments.

Message Map

The brand platform document should always serve as a roadmap for expression to various audience segments. Derived from the brand platform, a message map articulates the positioning statement in a context appropriate for each stakeholder audience or key segment, with slight variations to emphasize elements and language that will be most appealing and motivating to each group.

The expression of the positioning statement to motivate prospective undergraduates to enroll might differ slightly from the expression to appeal to adult and graduate students. Communication with law school, business school, and professional school stakeholders may be slightly different in emphasis from that targeting stakeholders in the arts, the humanities, and the sciences. An expression that motivates alumni engagement, participation, and advocacy might be related to, but different in terms of tone from, an expression to major donors and principal gift prospects.

The positioning statement that most speaks to athletic fans, supporters, and recruits certainly will not be the same as the appeal to faculty scholars that academic leaders hope to attract.

Just as a song has different verses that link back to the chorus via a bridge, every variation of the positioning statement must tie back to the overall positioning statement. It gets everyone singing from the same song sheet, as it were. The tone and personality of an expression might vary based on audience, but all should originate with the same small set of choices that are identified in the brand platform, which were informed by the research. Importantly, leaders' personal preferences in key areas should have little to do with the expression in those areas. Of course, the leaders should be comfortable with the expressions that are used in furtherance of the goals for which they are primarily accountable, and they will be if they helped to shape the underlying strategy and participated in its approval.

The message map can be derived with the CMO or agency partner, in partnership with the marketing task force, once the basic platform has been approved. The University of Buffalo has an excellent message map template and examples for specific audiences, such as graduate and professional education, on their website.[11]

Content Strategy

Building on the brand strategy, the strategic plan, and the message map, communicators use data about stakeholder audiences' needs, motivations, and goals to develop targeted plans for content on websites, on social media, and in other communication channels. Content strategy is defined as "the planning and judgment for the creation, publication, dissemination, and governance of useful, usable, effective content across departments and functional areas."[12]

More detail on content strategy is provided in chapter 7, but in a nutshell, the content is optimized for search and is regularly evaluated to tune performance in terms of search results, reinforcement of the institution's primary brand messages, and expression of the value proposition for each audience. In the most mature organizations, data are collected and analyzed at an individual-user level (consistent with appropriate privacy practices, terms, and conditions) so that communication and personalized future interactions can be tailored based on previous interactions with the institution and proactively offered. While the content strategy may be led by the CMO and appropriate designees, the plans can guide and integrate the work of communicators across the institution.

Bill Walker, a seasoned and experienced communication and marketing leader who has held the principal CMO role at multiple top-tier public and private institutions and tracked emerging trends to adapt in innovative ways over his entire career, says that one of the first places to embed content strategy, as well as the culture and technology needed to support it, is within the CMO's own domain. Walker has noticed that increasingly, sharp digital communication strategists are sitting right next to colleagues who employ very traditional communication practices (think media relations professionals who are all former journalists and creative services professionals who operate primarily in print).[13] Getting these professionals to think about how the content they create moves across platforms to be used and shared in multiple, integrated ways is one of the first steps in addressing integration. It can serve as a precursor to more enterprise-level content sharing and targeting.

Technology to Enable Integrated Platforms

It is difficult for communicators to share content that is in different formats and is stored in different technology solutions. Chapter 6, on digital marketing, covers the use of enterprise-level technologies, such as a content management system (CMS) to store, share, and serve up all web content and a customer relationship management (CRM) tool that records, schedules, and tracks all interactions with an individual, ideally across the student life-cycle, from point of first contact as a prospective student, through the student experience, to contact as alumna and donor after graduation. To the extent that the leadership works toward enterprise solutions for these functions, they are better equipped to facilitate integration of communication and experiences and develop greater insights that tie marketing activity to desired behaviors and outcomes.

Using Strategy and Best Practice to Avoid Pitfalls

Presidents and provosts must strike a deft and careful balance when they engage with leaders across the institution on topics that relate to marketing. Most do not want to use political capital to mediate disputes over logo use or color choice, nor should they.

When leaders behave in ways that demonstrate marketing as a strategic framework for building value, they open up a richer and more fundamental conversation about decisions that can reinforce the institution's differentiated position. Leaders also encourage the development of integrated marketing communication that expresses that position clearly, effectively, and repeatedly in ways that motivate many and varied stakeholders to act in supportive ways that build revenue and reputation.

Wise leaders set expectations and encourage integration by including the power users of the brand in building and choosing the overall brand strategy. They expect and cultivate trusting relationships among the executive team so that each member's primary goals are understood, shared, and embraced. They foster a culture that is open to making decisions that take into account the experiences of the individual stakeholder, and they seek to develop enterprise technology solutions that facilitate integration. Finally, they empower and support the CMO to employ tools of best practice, which put decisions about alignment and integration in a context of strategic marketing that is designed to be mutually beneficial.

Key Questions for Leaders and Their CMOs

- Do our decisions about product, price, and place align with our brand strategy?

- Do the experiences on our campuses, in our classrooms, and at our events align with our brand strategy?

- Has the entire campus embraced the brand? What does the brand mean for athletics, advancement, research, enrollment, etc.?

- Do leaders embed the brand platform into every touchpoint, speech, and written expression to university stakeholders?

Chapter 6

Digital U

Marketing Higher Education in a Digital World

Online, we all live in our own little personalized, precision targeted digi-worlds.

—Bob Hoffman, advertising executive

This chapter addresses topics that are, on their face, far more tactical, topics on which it makes little sense for institutional leaders to focus. That's where the CMO, the marketing team, and agency partners come in. However, to the extent that leaders need to understand the relative value of certain practices in order to support strategic investments and hold those who make them accountable for producing value, the chapter will familiarize leaders with practices, resources needed, and pitfalls to avoid. Terms are briefly defined to give leaders the language they need to ask informed questions and interpret results.

The subject of this chapter, digital marketing, is imbued by leaders with great hopes for less cost, more precise measurement, and more predictable results, most especially in terms of enrollment outcomes. There is good reason for such hopes, but only when the practice is demystified and when leaders avoid treating it as the quick and cheap silver bullet for all their recruitment challenges.

A strong brand strategy coupled with digital marketing, intensive recruitment practices, and content strategy can produce remarkable results. But those results are enabled by a significant investment in capacity that must be built or outsourced. The work is supported by strong, integrated technology platforms, software, and labor-intensive, targeted content creation, as well as constant monitoring, analysis, and refinement.

Digital marketing is not a practice for academic leaders to dabble in lightly or occasionally. It is a highly developed professional specialty, and its cost-effectiveness is only recognized at scale. There are good reasons why online program managers (OPMs), marketing services partners, and for-profit institutions focus on programs with high or growing market demand and great capacity for enrollment growth. Digital marketing tools make little economic sense for small-prospect pools or programs whose faculty refuse to allow more students to enroll. Leaders are wise to work with their academic, technology, and marketing leaders to consider which programs have the demonstrated demand or potential to support a strategic investment and then establish a roadmap for building or outsourcing the capacity to do this work.

Digital marketing and communication tools can be used to support strategic outcomes beyond enrollment. Alumni engagement and communication has become increasingly digital as the proportion of alumni who are digital natives has grown. Student success initiatives increasingly rely on many of the same technology platforms, analytical tools, and communication practices to produce desired retention and graduation results. Even donor engagement, communication, and stewardship practices are influenced by digital tools, especially for annual fund initiatives. Ticket sales for athletic, arts, and cultural events can all benefit from the segmentation and targeting that digital marketing enables.

All these practices were enabled by changes in technology that disrupted the ways in which we communicate and interact with others and make exchanges of value. Higher education is certainly not the first sector to reckon with this disruption, and many would argue that we are hanging on, tooth and nail, to outdated ways and outdated thinking. However, resistance hasn't prevented the disruption. Our expectations and those of our employees and stakeholders have been shaped by experiences in other sectors. How we get our news, interact with friends and family, date, exercise, shop, cook, eat, watch tv and movies, listen to music, sleep, work, pay bills, get help for home repairs, ride, travel, and vacation has been completely disrupted. Technology innovations have changed the way we make weekly offerings to our place of worship or make a sustaining gift to our favorite charity. This disruption has continued and accelerated with a necessary shift to virtual interactions during the 2020 coronavirus pandemic.

So of course technology has revolutionized where, when, and how students learn. How they seek information about learning options has changed too. Technology has revolutionized giving, engagement, advocacy, and support for favorite brands. The question for leaders is not whether to embrace this disruption but how best to employ it to build value. To influence the process, leaders should first understand the context in which stakeholders search, explore, and make decisions about exchanges of value using the internet.

The Context: A Student's Digital Journey

Where do students learn about institutions? While brand associations are often first formed through family, friends, teachers, colleagues, and media and cultural influences, specific information about an institution is likely to be accessed digitally. Here are the ways that students search and that institutions use digital tools to capture and address their interest.

Search

For traditional-age students, the first source is not the institution's website; it is far more likely to be videos on YouTube or Instagram or communities on Reddit. After consulting social media, they might check social forums such as College Confidential, where millions of posts by peers are considered trusted and authentic. They might search via a search engine (in all likelihood Google) to compare an institution with competitors. In the top search results, they will see comparisons of the institution with its closest competitors and with those with similar names—about which there might be confusion. Just below the top search results, they will see a feature Google offers called "People also ask," which presents the most commonly searched questions, such as "Is this a good school?" or "What kind of grade point average is required for admission?" Eventually, when traditional-age students do get around to accessing the institution's content, it is often more likely to be through social channels than through its home page, which might be a jumble of content for different audiences that is far too dense and lengthy to be of interest to a seventeen-year-old.

Search Assisted by Artificial Intelligence

Especially for adult students, the first explorations are likely to be shaped by Google, Siri, or Alexa, and their questions are addressed by search results optimized to answer them. "Alexa, where can I earn a master's degree in computer science?" "Siri, what does a nurse with a master's degree earn?" "Hey, Google, where can I take MBA classes on weekends or online?" Institutions engaged in digital marketing use their websites as hubs, with content optimized to anticipate and answer these questions so that it comes up first in organic search. Alternatively, institutions may pay to place relevant content, linked directly to specially designed web pages, at the top of the search results.

Landing Pages to Enable Tracking

When students click through links to institutional sites, a tiny, invisible bit of code installed on the web landing pages recognizes their computer or device. Through the use of *cookies* placed on students' web browsers, institutions can track and note the pages on which they land. That information will be stored and recalled to customize students' experience if they return to the page later, and it might also link to related searches on other pages, in email messages, or on social channels. (This information can be used to target and follow up later with students, even before they inquire, to offer digital content related to their previous searches. This might take the form of paid or sponsored content appearing on other pages the student visits or in the student's social channels, whether it looks like an ad or not.)

Requests for Information

In addition, the landing pages prominently feature a request for information (RFI), which, when completed, will allow the institution or its representative to follow up and begin to *qualify* interested students (sometimes called *leads*) and assess whether they are ready to apply. The information on the web landing page is often limited—just enough to pique interest—while also encouraging students to complete the RFI to get more information.

Chatbots

Mirroring the sales practice in other sectors, institutional websites are beginning to offer a *chatbot*, or an opportunity to interact with a customer service representative via text. A chatbot is an artificial intelligence tool connected to a knowledge base of content related to frequently asked questions. Both the chatbot and the customer service representative allow students to ask more specific questions right away and allow the institution to encourage completion of the RFI, so that they can establish an ongoing recruitment dialogue.

Search Beyond Enrollment

The search behavior described here is presented in the context of enrollment, but it extends to alumni and parent engagement and donor interests. Alumni might search for annual programs, athletic events, and local regional programs. Parents might seek information for a child struggling with academic adjustment, stress, or illness. Donors might want to know whether the institution is a good steward of philanthropic investments. Institutions that want to effectively engage their prospects and stakeholders anticipate these questions and seek to provide answers directly on web pages optimized with relevant content.

Those searching for information are on a journey to explore and engage in an exchange of value involving their time, money, or other support in return for something they seek. They are on a path to inquire, engage, or support the institution in some way. In crude terms, digital marketing tools are most often applied to initiate the "sales" part of this journey, identifying leads and focusing on those most likely and most qualified to move from exploration to action.

Some leaders find this following, tracking, and courting a bit creepy (and like boomers of a certain age, I did too, at first, given concerns about privacy), but digital natives aren't as likely to be put off, especially if the content being offered is relevant, authentic, and useful. However, it should be noted that when the content is not relevant or is unwelcome, they think it is spam, which underlines the importance of targeting. Further, note that rules for the collection and use of personal data of citizens of the European Union, known as the General Data Protection Regulation, require that institutions and organizations collecting data on EU citizens (through the use of cookies and RFIs) must post their policy on data privacy on their websites, where users opt in or out before using the site. This has resulted in many institutions across the globe reviewing and sharing their policy on personal data privacy, a trend that is likely to continue with increased scrutiny of major technology companies whose social and search platforms collect and sell data.

Can Digital Marketing Be Used for Brand Building?

Digital marketing practices that anticipate and answer potential customer questions with useful and relevant information are commonly referred to as *content* or *inbound marketing*, and their purpose is sales oriented—to move prospects or leads to express greater interest and eventually engage in an exchange of value. Brand marketing seeks to build name recognition, awareness, and differentiation from competitors. The two approaches can work together to form the basis for consideration so that when someone is ready to engage in an exchange of value, the institution is among those of interest.

Brand marketing can be achieved through digital and traditional forms of advertising. The appeal of digital marketing—targeted, trackable, with results easier to measure than those of traditional forms of marketing and advertising—causes many institutions to shift the balance of their investments to digital. "The reaction to changing media channels over the past decade and the rise of social media has been a slow walk from direct mail and print-based admissions to digital direct response," notes Jason Simon, CEO of SimpsonScarborough.[1] However, there's a risk in going all in on digital. Institutions that are not brand names may have inadvertently sidelined one of their most crucial priorities—brand building.

Here's why. Marketing through digital tools is necessarily narrow and targeted. Compared with other forms of brand advertising to build awareness through mass communication tools (print, display, broadcast, billboards, and mass transit), digital advertising is highly personalized, making it a private rather than a public experience. Many eyeballs notice outdoor advertising on a busy highway billboard. "Online, we all live in our own little personalized, precision targeted digi-worlds. This is not an environment conducive to growing brands," notes the advertising expert Bob Hoffman.[2] Simon suggests that for institutions that are not premium brands the balance of investment may have shifted too far toward digital. "Spending limited budgets solely on digital advertising and marketing won't build brand awareness and market penetration that's crucial to establishing long-term brand equity."[3]

For leaders of most institutions, then, the ease and appeal of measurement for digital should not solely drive decisions about investment. Rather, strategies, tactics, and measurement should be aligned with "what actually drives long-term, strategic, and all-encompassing brand equity: what do people think of your institution?"[4]

Know What You're Talking About: Digital Marketing Terms Defined

When leaders recognize how technology has changed the way that our prospects and stakeholders expect to learn about, evaluate, engage with, and develop relationships with all sorts of brands, including colleges and universities, they'd better understand how their marketing and communication teams or partners can and should influence that process. Familiarity with the following terms allows leaders to be more knowledgeable and adept in discussions about strategy, investments, and outcomes. Definitions and examples are provided to illustrate the nature and purpose of each.

SEO

Search engine optimization, or *SEO*, is a form of digital marketing that focuses on developing and publishing web content that is optimized to address the interests of target audiences, with the intent to make it rank highly in organic search results. The content is designed to be relevant, authoritative, and embedded with search terms that are likely to raise a web page's value in search algorithms, so that it is more likely to come near the top of a search results page. The more a page is accessed related to the common, relevant search terms, the higher the position in search results. Institutions that intentionally engage in SEO expect to see their results in search position improve. Generally, such efforts should aim for a position on the first page of search results, where the visibility generates the most web traffic, and the higher on the page, the better.

Content or *inbound marketing* is a practice designed to improve organic search position. It uses content to drive search users to the institution's relevant web page, where the goal is to convert a lead from interest to action. Blogs, podcasts, white papers, rankings, and articles that anticipate users' interests and answer their questions establish usefulness and relevance and lead potential customers to program pages for more information and calls to action.

In one of the most effective examples of higher education content marketing that I have ever seen, the online program manager 2U established a website providing the teacher certification requirements in all 50 US states in support of a new online master of arts in teaching at the University of Southern California. Previously, such information had been distributed in a different form in each state and was not available in one place. 2U collected and aggregated the information on an independent website, Teach.com. Aspiring teachers and current educators moving from one state to another who searched for "teacher certification requirements" in any state quickly started landing on the site. It filled a gap in terms of relevant information for current and aspiring teachers, who learned what they needed to fulfill requirements, which might include an advanced degree in education. The site was not branded as a USC site, but it prominently included an RFI about a master's degree in teaching that led to its degree program page. As a result, it generated interested leads in the online program and simultaneously elevated the position of the USC master's program in search rankings.

The benefits of SEO take time (think months) to develop, but they have a long-lasting effect if the efforts are sustained. There are few direct costs—it is not like paying for ads to generate leads. However, substantial tools and expert staff are required to gather and analyze data on target audiences; to develop, test, optimize, and maintain relevant content to generate a high position in search; and to develop inbound content marketing to drive traffic. Unfortunately, web content publishing at colleges and universities is widely distributed among staff and faculty who are not experts in SEO and who are not trained to optimize web content or to use analytical tools that evaluate and improve website performance. While there might be expert leadership in digital strategies in the CMO's or CIO's office, there may not be the kind of focus or bandwidth to do this work well except on the highest-level institutional web pages. Often, a digital marketing agency, an SEO consultant, or an OPM partner may be hired to focus on sustained institutional or program-specific search engine results.

SEM

Search engine marketing, or *SEM*, also known as paid search, is a form of digital marketing that promotes websites by increasing their visibility on search engine results pages through paid advertising rather than relying on a high earned position from organic search. SEM is often used to quickly establish and promote a branded program while SEO strategies are being developed over time to establish a high position in organic search results.

Advertisers pay search engine companies like Google for keywords—actually, they bid for them—and pay per click when a user clicks on the ad. The process of identifying and bidding for relevant keywords to maximize the marketing budget is complex and can be affected not only by the relevance of the content on the institution's landing page but also by competitors, whose budgets might be higher. Competitors' bids for keywords may drive the cost upward. The ideal keywords provide the most leads for the least cost. Members of the CMO's team can assist with this process, but often program-specific SEM is outsourced to experts at agencies or partners working on behalf of the institution.

Owned, Earned, and Paid Media

Digital marketing investments can be distributed among owned, earned, and paid media channels. Marketers seek to leverage each for greater overall effectiveness in a digital marketing program.

Owned media are institutional web properties, like websites, blogs, e-newsletters, and social media channels, that are home to digital content controlled by the college or university, places where it represents and extends its brand. Owned media channels are the ultimate destination for links from earned and paid media. Increased inbound links from those channels to the institution's own content help improve its position in organic search.

Earned media are the digital equivalent of word of mouth. They demonstrate authentic interest from others, including reviews, recommendations, mentions, reposts, shares, and content picked up by third party sites. Earned media help to drive brand sentiment and loyalty. Digital marketers use content strategy and SEO to inspire and influence prospects through support on earned media. Content developed by the institution and high search position puts the institution's owned media in a more likely position to be visited and shared.

Paid media are ads and content that are sponsored or paid for and drive users to earned and owned media. For institutions or programs that do not enjoy brand awareness or strong search positions, paid media ads get things started. All forms of digital advertising fall into this category, including pay-per-click (PPC), display ads, retargeting, paid content promotion, social media ads, and content produced by paid influencers. Leaders can rely on their CMOs or agencies to provide more information on how these tools work, as well as the resources and capacity necessary to make them effective.

Developing the Capacity to Support Digital Marketing

A host of technology tools, professional expertise, and human resources are necessary to follow up on and cultivate leads generated from digital marketing to make the effort successful and produce value. This capacity must be built internally, outsourced to agencies or partners, or some hybrid of both. Leaders often struggle with where this capacity should reside in the institution, who should be responsible and accountable, and what level of investment to make. Perhaps part of the struggle is realizing that the capacity represents a sales force (the related industry-leading software is so named for good reason), a function for which few academic organizations have a natural affinity. Nevertheless, if the sales capacity to follow up on leads doesn't exist, the investment in digital marketing will be wasted—a mistake I have unfortunately witnessed repeatedly, as academic leaders grasped for the short-term action without effectively following through on the back end. Even more frustrating, such experiences lead academic leaders to conclude that digital marketing doesn't work rather than recognizing that it must be properly applied to programs with the scale to support the investment and that it must be met with recruitment capacity to finish the job that marketing starts.

The challenges of building and managing this capacity are part of the reason why OPMs are able to negotiate the lion's share of revenue when they contract to build an online program for a college or university. A tour of the 2U headquarters several years ago revealed a finely tuned marketing and recruitment operation, with a talented inbound marketing team, strong analytics and SEO approaches, and a humming center with hundreds of employees, dedicated to daily and weekly sales goals to convert leads to applicants, and applicants to enrolling students, for their many partner institutions. Calls, emails, texts, and video chats were scheduled and completed in a carefully sequenced workflow, designed to find and focus on the leads most likely to enroll. A Huffington Post article in 2019 noted that 19 percent of revenue for a 2U program went to digital marketing and recruitment expenses,[5] which signals the huge upfront cost necessary to produce strong net revenue, especially for new programs.

It is possible that as digital strategies for online learning, student success, and marketing and recruiting become more mature on college campuses, the internal capacity to support them will develop and become part of the basic infrastructure of the institution. In the meantime, OPMs and digital marketing services are starting to disaggregate their services and offer à la carte options so that as institutions build some capacity, they can complement it with outsourced expertise and staffing.

The global research and advisory firm Gartner's 2019 Marketing Organizational Survey reported that 63 percent of marketers (across all industry sectors) had moved some aspects of their delivery from third-party agencies to in-house teams, though spending on marketing agencies still accounted for nearly a quarter (22%) of total marketing budgets. "While in-housing may be à la mode, agencies still offer an unparalleled breadth of scope, economies of scale and an ability to offer much-needed, external strategic input," said Ewan McIntyre at Gartner. At the same time, marketing technology investments had dropped three percentage points since 2018, falling to 26 percent of marketing budgets in 2019. While this technology still commands a major slice of the marketing budget, it has proved to be a more volatile investment area. Gartner's survey revealed that "24% of marketers believe martech strategy, adoption and use is one of their top three weaknesses in their company's ability to drive customer acquisition or loyalty. More than 25% of marketers blame those martech strategy weaknesses on insufficient budget, resources or capabilities."[6]

Here, then, is a basic review of the elements that leaders should recognize as necessary so that they can determine whether the investment in capacity should be made internally or outsourced. It may be wise to start with a pilot, using a high-capacity program with high market interest, and acquire the outsourced capacity to start out. Watch and learn how the external partner organizes, implements, and evaluates the work. If the pilot is successful or promising, then a roadmap can be developed to determine how to gradually bring some or all of the capacity in house if the expertise exists internally or can be hired.

Technology

Institutions need tools to manage their digital content, develop and schedule interactions with prospects, and test and optimize the effectiveness of both content and efforts. CMOs and CIOs possess critical expertise that should inform decisions about appropriate investment in and implementation of these tools. The basics include:

- A content management system, which hosts the institution's web content. Since many institutions developed their internet presence organically, unit by unit, independent decisions about CMS were made, so it is not uncommon for one university to have many CMS systems in use. When institutions don't have an enterprise-wide CMS, managing, developing, and sharing content, which is at the root of all digital marketing strategy and the associated content strategy, is more challenging. Finding ways to integrate CMS systems or migrating to support of one enterprise CMS is critical to healthy functioning in the digital environment.

- Digital asset management tools, which store, organize, and provide ready access to media, including video and photography.
- Customer relationship management software, which helps to manage the institution's relationships with current and prospective customers. It is designed to record interactions at all key touchpoints and develop insights and intelligence to improve outcomes and experience. The tool establishes prospect records at the earliest expression of interest, tracks and helps to manage steps to cultivate relationships, organizes the workflow related to all communication and contact, and records the responses and outcomes. In the ideal state, one enterprise CRM facilitates relationships over the entire student lifecycle, from recruitment through enrollment and as engaged alumni. This is common in corporate organizations and OPMs but uncommon in higher education.
- Marketing automation software, which is designed to streamline, automate, and measure the effectiveness of marketing and recruitment sequences (emails, texts, social media interactions) with prospects. Customized workflows prepared for key market segments automate a schedule of communication with prospects who have responded to digital marketing campaigns or initiated requests for information. Because effective "sales" work is so labor intensive, these systems are designed to work with CRMs and reduce reliance on human labor.
- Analytical tools, such as Google Analytics, heat maps, and SEO tools, to segment, target, and track potential and current stakeholders or customers and gain insights on their experiences.

Data Analytics and Market Research Expertise

Marketing professionals rely on analysts who interpret and provide insights on customer experience, lead and evaluate SEO performance, and use predictive analytics to focus on those most likely to convert to the next level of engagement, to estimate market demand for programs to which these tools might be applied, and to divide audiences into targeted segments for customized marketing plans. Data analysts, in particular, are in great demand and command some of the highest salaries in marketing organizations, and their expertise is becoming increasingly critical. Market demand and SEO expertise may be accessed through agencies.

Recruitment, Follow-up, and Customer Satisfaction and Retention

Those who cultivate personal relationships with prospects and use the CRM to track and record interactions with them are the sales force of staff. Their days (or nights, in the case of work with adult students) are spent calling, emailing, texting, and messaging prospects, gauging their interest, responding to questions, advising them on next steps, and encouraging them to engage. In some organizations, they or other staff advisors continue the relationship during enrollment to enhance satisfaction and retention. Southern New Hampshire University, for example, discovered through data analysis that successful completion of six online courses was a key predictor of retention, so it maintained a staff of advisors to continue relationships with students, aided by the CRM, to coach them through this critical period.

Retaining staff who are trained in the use of the CRM is another challenge that institutions face. Like data analysts, these staff are in demand both within and outside higher education. They usually are assigned to a program, a market segment, or a territory. When they are on leave, their work must be covered, and they must be promptly replaced if they depart; otherwise there will be an immediate negative effect on workflow and outcomes in the assigned area. At American, for digital recruitment of graduate students for master's degree programs we developed a group of assigned CRM specialists (one for each school or college), as well as two enterprise-level specialists who could move to cover an area during an absence or departure. In addition, developing use of the CRM beyond the most basic level is another challenge to realizing its full capacity.

Content Strategy and Execution

Content strategy is "the planning and judgement for the creation, publication, dissemination, and governance of useful, usable, effective content across departments and functional areas."[7] It may seem obvious at first, and then eventually daunting, that according to this definition content is every item produced for an organization's key audiences—every word, image, or medium, every story, article, white paper, research presentation, lecture, social media post, photograph, video, graphic design, podcast, and so on. Ideally, content informed by data is created and delivered at just the right time in just the right way to the right audience member. Such content feeds SEO and paid digital marketing efforts to identify new customers and engages and satisfies existing stakeholders.

When it comes to leveraging content to reinforce institutional identity and brand, a lack of coordination works against clear and compelling communication. At best, content producers within campus communities are open to sharing content, but they may be oblivious to content in other departments that is duplicative or contradictory. At worst, they are competitive and protective of their content. Neither situation facilitates coordination of content to support a more compelling story aligned with an overarching brand position.

Tim Jones, former chief communication and integrated marketing officer at Beloit College, repeats a story that every CMO recognizes. At any given moment, a faculty member, trustee, or academic leader considering how to address enrollment, fundraising, or reputational challenges may suggest, "We just need to do a better job of telling our story." As Jones points out, "Almost simultaneously comes the faint sound of higher education marketers and content creators everywhere joining in a collective face-palm."[8]

Of course, a lot of content is already being thoughtfully created, but academic cultures and systems do not provide the conditions for easy coordination around stories that are strategically focused on brand alignment and informed by data about the audiences of interest. And as Jones notes, even the most thoughtfully crafted content aligned with the brand and audience interests fails to capture the full story of the people, place, and experiences our institutions offer because "it is not just what you say and how you say it."[9] Since brands are the sum total of all experiences with an institution, they live in the minds of constituents, and every audience interaction shapes perceptions. Integrated marketing, which seeks to align communication, experiences, and institutional decisions with the core brand promise, is an institution's best hope for telling a better story and living up to the story it tells.

So how do institutions begin to adopt a more intentional content strategy that facilitates coordination and eventually integration? A study of professional associations was the basis for development of a model of content strategy maturity. This model revealed that organizations in the early stages of adopting a content strategy focused on tactical measures to begin coordinating their content.[10] As the content strategy advances and the organization matures in its use, the focus is more integrated and strategic, which, as Jones suggests, is the point at which not only communication but experiences are aligned with the overall institutional brand. Culture and leadership play a role in developing buy-in for content strategy and fostering mature use over time.

Tools to Encourage and Facilitate Content Coordination Aligned with Brand

Institutions at the early stages of a journey to adopt a content strategy are focused on more tactical coordination. The tools to effect this coordination include content audits, brand platform documents, message maps, and personas, as well as training and incentives for faculty and staff who create content related to enrollment, fundraising, and positioning. CMOs or agency partners should provide leadership and governance to deploy these tools and share their relevance with leaders.

From Content Coordination to Mature, Integrated Marketing

To go beyond coordination of communication, leaders orient their planning and decision-making to align with the brand strategy. Jones initiated a series of leadership initiatives at Beloit College that were designed to help senior leaders do so.

> We've oriented senior staff in working groups designed to explore and implement answers to questions about how we do our work that will significantly impact business outcomes through an integrated marketing approach. . . . We're looking at things like how we can resource, design, use and activate spaces on campus to signal and advance our values; how campus visits, both programmatically and experientially, can better shape audience understanding of our value proposition; how our academic product reflects our values and can best serve our audiences; and how our digital presence can create demand for the college. Integrated marketing clearly marks the intersections of these questions and provides a consistent way to answer.[11]

Such an approach elevates the support for the brand from content strategy to truly integrated marketing. Institutions that reach this level of integration increase the likelihood that all the ways its stories are told and experiences are formed are in service of alignment with the brand strategy. And further, communicators supporting the efforts to shape facilities, campus visits, academic programs, and digital presence are more likely to be aligned in purpose, not just coordinated in their communication.

Content to Support Specific Programs

If developing and coordinating effective content for digital marketing to support the institution's overall brand strategy is a common institutional challenge, the challenges multiply at the program level. The quantity and demand for timely, fresh, and targeted content increase with the addition of each program. Digital marketing machines like OPMs and Southern New Hampshire University deploy internal or agency writers, designers, editors, and analysts to create, test, deliver, and evaluate content for owned and paid media in order to fulfill this ongoing need. All the content is developed by professionals who work within an overarching brand platform and create interesting content that is suitably tailored to the audience segment of interest.

At American University, our failure to adequately identify and fund a dedicated capacity for content generation was one of the key reasons that our internal digital marketing efforts for graduate programs were not successfully sustained. In our early pilot of digital marketing for a small number of master's programs, we successfully developed tools that facilitated a focus on effective communication with prospective graduate students. Faculty program directors and current graduate students responded well to the training and to tools such as personas, which allowed them to describe their programs in compelling and effective ways. The content generated by faculty and current students was the most informed and authentic, effectively representing the program and generating real interest. Yet those same faculty and students had many other responsibilities beyond generating content for digital marketing of their program, so that over time they could not sustain their content responsibilities in a reliable or timely manner.

It was not as though the dedicated capacity for content creation had not been anticipated. Indeed, a team of academic and administrative leaders developed a roadmap that showed all the capacities that would be necessary to build and sustain an internal digital marketing capacity, including all the elements identified in the previous chapter. However, one element of the roadmap—content generation—was always met with the same reaction. With limited resources to invest in a host of priorities (CRM tools and staff, a call center, website development, marketing strategy, media buying, analytics), content generation always fell to the bottom of the list. The common refrain, from the Budget Office to the Office of Graduate Studies, was that we had dozens of resources not just in the central marketing office but in the colleges and schools, whose responsibilities included communication. Why couldn't they be deployed to support this content need? The reality, of course, was that those communication professionals were dedicated to developing content for a host of other priorities, ranging from the university's brand to the positioning of particular colleges and schools, and to communication with other important audiences, including alumni, current students, and donors. Weighing against the notion of reallocating some of those resources toward digital marketing of a specific program were the political cost and the difficulty of altering the organizational structure or reporting lines in support of more efficiency, coordination, or dedicated capacity.

For some small master's programs, we experimented with an alternative resource that would avoid reliance on the faculty, staff, and students for regular content generation as well as outreach and recruitment management. We hired an outside marketing and recruitment services firm. Their efforts to generate program content, as well as their interactions with prospective students, were more reliable and productive, but their representations of the program were seen by its faculty and students as less authentic and less accurate than those previously produced internally. Moreover, the number of inquiries, applications, and enrollments, while equal to the number in previous years, was not sufficient to cover the cost of the outsourced services. The cost of acquisition was high and not covered by net tuition. In fairness, the firm made clear that the cost of acquisition made more sense for larger programs with sufficient market demand and enrollment capacity.

The lessons of these experiments helped us learn about the obstacles that had to be surmounted in order to develop the necessary capacity for program-specific content strategy. What was required for both programs was a resource that would become trusted and expert in the specifics of each and dedicated to creating and formatting content that would be of interest to prospective students. Further, applying such resources would only make sense if the programs had the demand and enrollment capacity to warrant the expense. Ultimately, the failure to provide dedicated and informed content resources was a critical gap that proved fatal to a sustained internal digital marketing program.

Considerations for Leaders

For institutions who have invested in a brand strategy, it makes sense to take stock of the content for priority audiences through an audit and to empower the CMO and the marketing team or agency to employ some of the tools mentioned in this chapter to encourage and incentivize coordination and integration of content, as well as to assume responsibility for standards and governance. Presidents and their executive teams may welcome planning and decision-making frameworks that encourage making strategic choices while keeping the brand strategy and the needs of key stakeholder priorities foremost in their minds.

For program-specific marketing, externally provided content resources should be applied only to larger programs with the scale to make the cost of acquisition reasonable, and even then, training, regular review, and quality control must be in place to ensure that the external firm's representation of the program is in alignment with the institution's brand. For smaller programs, and in instances where the content is internally generated, the resources must be dedicated to ensuring that content is accurate, authentic, and reliably produced.

The challenges of adopting a content strategy are numerous, especially given the culture of higher education institutions, which tend to be decentralized, autonomous, and therefore uncoordinated. However, to fulfill the expectations of stakeholders and build value through satisfying exchanges, leaders play important roles in encouraging coordination of content through tactical tools, making decisions to reinforce integration through communication and experiences, and identifying dedicated and informed capacity for programs of sufficient scale when such investments makes sense.

Setting Reasonable Expectations and Avoiding Pitfalls

Among the most important takeaways for leaders are that digital marketing tools and strategies by themselves do not build value. They must be accompanied by sales and recruitment capacity that follows up when initial interest is expressed, and that capacity has not been successfully built within most institutions of higher education. Institutions with robust online programs, OPMs, and digital marketing agencies have such capacity, which can be accessed, but it will eat into a proportion of the value generated.

Moreover, this work is not something amateurs should dabble in. Professional expertise by competitors doing it well will trump immature or ill-informed efforts. CMOs and CIOs should be leading the decisions about how to build or secure capacity and expertise. Outside partners should be solicited and evaluated with marketing and technology expertise at the table. Outside partners should be accountable for deliverables, and the institutions should have options to adjust or end the partnership in a timely manner if goals are not achieved.

In addition, reasonable expectations about measurement must be set. Yes, digital marketing provides more ability to track and measure the response of potential customers. However, because higher education technology tools are deployed unevenly, poorly integrated, and disparately managed, it is quite difficult to tie a particular marketing tactic to a particular outcome. Even in organizations that have enterprise software and better-integrated systems, measurement is most effective when tactics are evaluated in terms of the next expected outcome or behavior. Evaluating the click-through rate for a display ad relative to industry and regional norms is appropriate, but showing that the ad was the main or the only reason a student filled out a request for information is difficult. At best, tracking mechanisms determine the *last* place on the web that a user came from (the referring page) before they came to the landing page and requested more information. Often, however, prospects see an ad with a call to action multiple times, in addition to searching, inquiring, and taking time to consider whether to provide their information in an RFI. This is the problem of multiple source attribution, which marketing automation software aims to address with more precision, but it is still an elusive goal.

Julia Zito, assistant vice-president for marketing at American University, reminds colleagues that the time it takes for a student to make a decision to pursue a degree is significant; the consideration is more careful than for other buying decisions, given the level of time and money invested. Zito calls this the resumé commitment: very few choices based on decisions about products or services will end up on a resumé and be there for the rest of one's career.[12] Thus, prospects may see and be influenced by digital marketing over time, long before they ever decide to act. Identifying all the points of contact with a given prospect, prior to identification through the RFI, is impossible, and determining which of the known contacts or impressions was the greatest influence is fraught with assumptions that our technology tools have yet to surmount.

Determining the influence of an ad or a piece of content on the decision to apply and enroll is even more fraught. Many other influences affect the decision to apply and enroll, including all the sales and recruitment activity (or lack thereof), offers of financial aid or discounts, net price, offers made by competitors, and perceptions of brand quality and reputation. Digital marketing activity in the enrollment context is designed to affect the top stages of the funnel, click-throughs to landing pages and leads or inquiries. Outcomes at the middle and bottom of the funnel are influenced by other factors, so application and enrollment decisions are not reasonable measures of activity at the top—digital marketing. To the extent that the activities at the top yield qualified and interested leads, and enough of them to generate prospects that will in the end produce desired enrollments, fair enough. A holistic evaluation of the prospect funnel is a better one, measuring the impact of all the known marketing and recruitment activities that affect the outcomes, to the extent that these can be accurately tracked and attributed.

In this chapter, we reviewed requirements and considerations for building digital marketing capacity, including expertise, strategy, tools, and measurement, providing a natural segue to the broader topic of marketing measurement.

Key Questions for Leaders and Their CMOs

- Are we paying close attention to the customer's digital journey? Do we have the tools and infrastructure necessary to deliver a seamless experience?

- Are our digital marketing efforts keeping up with the latest trends? if not, why not?

- What is our infrastructure for data analysis and market research? Is it sufficient?

- Do we have a content strategy that spans audiences and channels to effectively "tell our story"?

Chapter 7

Measuring Results and Progress

I can't say cause and effect—it's like a lot of investment in market-ing and communication. I can point to proxy measures such as huge increases in the number of people who have turned up at our open days, huge satisfaction levels at these events, good conversion statistics and increasing numbers of students in a more competitive market.

—Sir David Bell, vice-chancellor, University of Reading,
United Kingdom

Since market research is the foundation of brand strategy, the measurement of results should be tightly linked to the strategy and the research that informed it. A measurement plan should be developed in the early stages of establishing or refining a marketing plan. It should be the rigorous basis upon which out-comes are monitored, interpreted, and faithfully reported to leadership, the marketing task force, and other stakeholders and constituencies in order to build and maintain support for the plan and associated investment, and to guide necessary changes or adjustments.

Leaders are advised to pack their patience for this journey. Results associated with brand strategy are likely to become evi-dent slowly over time because they are often associated with changes in human perception—something that rarely changes quickly. The process is often passive and gradual unless external events intervene.[1] Only in instances when an institution has badly shocked the public and disappointed its stakeholders, or in even more rare circumstances when an institution wildly exceeds expectations in a very concrete and relatable way, do perceptions change more quickly. Think of the Cinderella team in the finals of a national athletic championship tournament, or a faculty's first Nobel Prize winner, whose work is widely recognized and whose impact is easily understood. Even in these instances of rapid change in perceptions the negative or positive effects may be short-lived. However, in most instances, people do not track an institution's brand as closely as its own leaders and internal stakeholders do, so perceptions remain stable over time unless people are regularly and repeatedly given new information that challenges an old perception.

Leaders investing in smart brand strategies can expect small, steady, incremental changes that last over the long term, reflecting changes in awareness, favorability, or perceptions of quality, for example. In the short and middle term, measures can track the predicates for these long-term changes, including, for example, recall of primary brand messages or association of brand qualities that were chosen as primary differentiators.

Changes in behaviors associated with brand support or brand loyalty can also be tracked, since these reflect a shift in perceptions before the perceptions themselves are actually observed or measured. These are outcomes that leaders are most interested in changing. For example, increases in inquiries, applications, yield rates, retention, annual giving, and dollars raised can all reflect the influence of successful brand strategies. However, such changes can be influenced by many other factors, so discerning the impact of branding changes compared with that of other changes is nearly impossible.

In most instances, leaders don't make institutional changes in an experimental design, in which there is both a control group and a treatment group and in which only one change at a time is introduced that could affect the desired outcome. More likely than not, leaders will make as many changes in practice as possible that might positively impact strategic outcomes and live with the reality that the influence of various factors is not easily sorted out. Sir David Bell, vice-chancellor of the University of Reading, in the United Kingdom, notes the importance of these "proxy measures," even if the influences of marketing and other influences can't be cleanly sorted.

> Though in some cases, I can't say cause and effect—it's like a lot of investment in marketing and communication. I can point to proxy measures such as huge increases in the number of people who have turned up at our open days, huge satisfaction levels at these events, good conversion statistics and increasing numbers of students in a more competitive market.
>
> I also think that our positioning . . . had an effect on research income as we've grown. We've attracted things we never attracted before—major national and international partners. Again, I can't say cause and effect. But I think I would say we weren't out there blowing our own trumpet previously.
>
> As parts of the university have seen the quality of what we are doing through this process, they've noticed that it was better than what had gone previously. It helped that most of the proxy measures were going in the right direction as well.[2]

In a nutshell, if the elements of the brand strategy are designed to change perceptions that will yield greater awareness, support, and loyalty, then the change in associated behaviors should be in the right direction over time. If there is no change in important proxy measures, or if the direction of change is negative over a period of more than two years, then it is reasonable to conclude that adjustments to the implementation of the strategy are necessary.

In this chapter, measures to evaluate the impact of brand marketing for the short, middle, and long term are suggested, framed in terms of the larger strategic outcomes that such plans are designed to influence.

Preparing for Rigorous Measurement

Robert Moore and Tom Abrahamson provide an excellent roadmap for establishing a rigorous measurement program. The roadmap starts by identifying the measures an institution expects brand marketing to influence. They advocate collecting and monitoring a series of institutional metrics, including enrollment and fundraising measures, to establish a baseline for current performance and continuing to monitor those metrics on an institutional dashboard. "The development of a baseline of current performance is a critical first step in establishing the value of your marketing operation."[3] Without baseline data to show where the institution started, Robert Sevier points out, "it will be very difficult to evaluate progress."[4]

Setting a Baseline for Ongoing Proxy Measures

The metrics for institutions may vary according to the strategic goals they expect to influence through marketing strategy and investments. If one considers the many ways that institutions build value, depending on key audiences and strategic goals, the metrics could extend beyond enrollment and fundraising. Broadly speaking, these performance measures might fall into several categories:

- Recruitment and enrollment metrics
  - Markets, suspects, prospects, applicants, admits, matriculants, discount rate, net tuition, retention
- Alumni engagement metrics
  - Volunteer, experiential, philanthropic, and communication[5]
- Development metrics
  - Annual giving, capital/endowment support, including number of gifts and dollars
- Research support
  - Grants and contracts, research expenditures, federal R&D

- Legislative engagement/support metrics
  - Advocacy activity, capital projects, state allocations
- Business and community engagement/support
  - Partnerships, bond ratings, neighbor engagement

Tracking and monitoring performance of key measures on a dashboard that reflects at least annual changes allows leaders to monitor those outcomes that should be influenced by marketing to build value. For an institution just beginning to invest in brand strategy, the baseline should be the performance for the year before the investments were made.

At American University, we annually tracked several measures as proxies for growing awareness and greater brand strength. Before we launched our brand strategy, the yield rate, or conversion of admitted students to enrolled first-year students, was 19.5 percent. (In fact, when making the case for investment of brand resources, especially to internal audiences, I used this as the basis for a cost-effectiveness argument. The substantial resources invested to recruit and admit a class of enrolled first-year students was yielding only one in five. If AU could increase its brand strength to the level of that of competitor institutions and aspirational peers, we might yield one in three admitted students or even three out of five. A more productive yield rate would more than pay for the investment in marketing.) Two years after the brand strategy was introduced, the yield rate had ticked up almost three points, and within seven years it had reached 33.5 percent, or one in three admitted students enrolled.

Another measure we tracked from baseline was the percentage of enrolled first-year students who identified AU as their first choice. (These data originate from a survey administered to first-year students at participating institutions in the earliest weeks of their college career, the CIRP Freshman Survey, led by the Higher Education Research Institute at UCLA.)[6] Before we implemented the strategy, fewer than half (44.7%) indicated that

AU was their top choice. Institutions with stronger brands, including competitors, had percentages representing strong majorities who preferred the institution in which they enrolled—three-quarters or more at the institutions with very strong brands. In the years after the brand strategy was launched, we watched the percentage zigzag and climb to 61 percent. Here, a word of caution is called for regarding volatile proxy measures. From year to year we would see the percentage for whom AU was the first choice rise or fall by several percentage points. However, the clear trajectory over several years was upward. If a measure is less stable from year to year, it is a good idea for leaders to set expectations and focus on whether the trend is directionally correct over the longer term.

A third proxy we used at AU in the first years of the brand strategy related to the goal of greater engagement of alumni. For a host of reasons—including AU's maturity in advancement work relative to competitors, as well as an extended and highly publicized leadership and governance crisis in the years that preceded the brand strategy—many alumni were not regularly engaged with the institution. In concert with the vice-president of development and alumni relations, we tracked an alumni engagement index, which measured the frequency of weighted measures of engagement, including alumni participation, volunteer engagement and leadership, and giving. Three years after the brand strategy was launched, alumni engagement had nearly tripled.

Finally, while we assiduously avoided overall rankings in *US News & World Report*'s Best Colleges guide as a proxy measure—because it was a volatile year-to-year measure, often subject to the editor's latest changes in methodology—we did focus on the peer assessment score of higher education leaders. This is a notoriously stable indicator, not likely to change much from year to year. Even small changes in the ratings of peers had (until recently, when its overall weight diminished relative to other factors) strong relative impact on the overall score. More importantly, for AU it represented a documented lack of awareness, with most leaders assigning it a rating in the middle of the five-point Likert scale, at 2.9, for many years. Based on interviews with peer leaders, we surmised that this was the equivalent of a "don't know much except the name," damning AU to the middle of the scale and the back of the pack in the overall ratings of the top 100 national universities. Leaders at peer and aspirational competitors became a priority audience for our marketing and communication strategies, and over several years the score rose slowly from 2.9 to 3.0, 3.1, and eventually 3.2. This contributed to a rise in the overall ranking, from 84 at the baseline to a high mark of 69, until recent changes diminished the weight of the peer assessment of academic reputation in favor of other new factors.

Setting the Baseline for Long-Term Measures

The initial stakeholder research that informs a brand strategy also provides the discipline for rigorous measurement. The findings that shape the goals of the brand strategy should become the baseline measures for progress over time.

For example, many institutions investing in brand strategy are focused on establishing awareness among target audiences, and for good reason. Audiences must recognize the institution and its key differentiators or brand associations in order to consider it among competitive alternatives that will be evaluated for possible engagement and support. Moreover, as Richard Taylor, chief operating officer at Loughborough University, in the United Kingdom, demonstrated, awareness is directly related to strong reputation. "Having a strong reputation and being known for things are the same thing. If people believe you have a strong reputation, they will also believe that they know things about you. Vice versa, if people do not believe they know things about your organisation, they will also believe you have a weak reputation. There's no third way."[7] Taylor illustrated this point with data from surveys of opinion leaders and consumers, who rated the reputations of British universities with which they were familiar or responded "don't know" for those with which they were not familiar. Taylor noted that the correlation between reputation score and "don't know" was very strong, and in the case of the consumer survey, .97. He concluded, "Being known for things is the way to build a strong reputation."[8]

Awareness can be measured through the institution's own market research, by asking target audiences to name excellent institutions in a region or market (unaided awareness) or by asking them to rate their familiarity with the institution and key competitors or to identify key associations. For example, "When you think of American University, what three things come to mind?" Establishing the baseline familiarity relative to that of competitors and asking for key associations allows an institution to track progress over time. To continue with the example at American, our stakeholder studies, including the baseline and two replications in subsequent years, demonstrated gains in familiarity relative to competitors. The first study showed how many prospective students, their parents, and peer leaders knew little about the institution. Later, in the second and third studies, most audiences associated messages from the brand campaign with the institution. It was gratifying to compare the word clouds from the first study, which seemed relatively sparse (for lack of awareness and differentiators), with those from the second and third studies, which were far more dense and detailed, with answers like "DC," "politics," "international," "diversity," and "wonk" coming through loud and clear to the question, "What comes to mind when you think of AU?" Similarly gratifying, in the second study, three years after the brand launch, "Things you associate with a wonk" frequently yielded the responses "knowledgeable," "smart," "passionate," "expert," "political," and even "American University," all messages from the campaign, although in full disclosure, and keeping us humble, "nerdy" and "don't know" still came up in some responses.

In addition to awareness, favorability or perceptions of reputation might be tested in the baseline research, and if these are the basis for goals in the brand strategy, they should be tracked and retested among audiences over time. Similarly, if differentiation among competitors is the desired goal, then unaided or aided recall of differentiators might be the subject of baseline measures and retests. If brand loyalty and satisfaction are of interest, then setting the benchmark for Net Promoter Scores by audience or segment will be important. The Net Promoter Score, or NPS, is a simple score derived by asking customers to rate their likelihood of recommending an institution to a friend or colleague on a scale of 0 to 10.[9] Those who responded 0-6 are detractors, those who respond 7-8 are passives, and those who respond 9-10 are promoters. The percentage of detractors is subtracted from the percentage of promoters, and the result is expressed as a percentage, ranging from −100 to 100. Strong brands have fewer detractors and passive stakeholders and more promoters, and thus higher NPS scores. Progress with target audiences and relative to competitors can be tracked over time.

The key to choosing among these measures is to consider what outcomes are the focus of the brand strategy and to track them over the middle and long term.

Asking the Big Question

Sevier points out that no matter what goals are to be achieved through marketing strategy, the overall outcome should be evaluated in part by answering this question: "Has the financial condition of the college or university improved since it began marketing?" Granted, the question is overly simplistic and, as Sevier suggests, even crass in the eyes of some. Yet, if we are operating from the assumption that marketing is a strategic function that builds value, how can one not consider the overall financial situation? "Most marketing goals have as their logical end the improvement of the college or university's financial condition. . . .

One way to measure the overall effectiveness of your marketing plan is to see whether the institution is better off afterward than before."[10] A reasonable measure could be derived in partnership with the CFO and might include annual net revenue or net assets, for example.

Moore and Abrahamson also advocate a measure that calculates the lifetime value of students and alumni, which can be estimated from other measures.[11] The lifetime revenue generated by a class of entering students can be estimated on the basis of measures including annual tuition and fees and average discount rate to determine a gross per-student revenue. The total is a staggering amount: for a private institution with 10,000 undergraduates enrolled, an average rate of tuition and fees, and an average discount rate, one could expect the lifetime value of a class entering in 2013 to be more than $221 million over four years. At a public institution of 20,000 students, the lifetime value of one class of students was estimated to be more than $209 million. Similarly, the lifetime value of a class of graduating alumni can be estimated using data on average gift size and giving rates, multiplied by the average number of years that they give. Such eye-popping value starts to put into perspective the investments made in marketing, and the measures can be tracked as trends related to building institutional value.

Short-Term Measures

In addition to tracking outcomes that are proxy measures for signs of trends or progress, it is wise to generate a list of measures or trends that reflect awareness or recognition of the brand expression. What measures indicate that the messages are registering? Anything that reflects pickup, early interest, or engagement can be useful. If a digital or social tactic is employed at launch, then hits to a website, click-through rates from email or paid ads, or engagement on social channels might be good early indicators. Media coverage should be monitored, though expect journalists to include comments from both supporters and detractors to reflect balance; in my experience, with a few notable exceptions, they tend to start with a jaundiced view of marketing as "spin." Expressions of sentiment in media and on social channels can be monitored, though again, strong sentiment—positive or negative—is more prevalent than neutrality in those expressions.

Don't underestimate the power of signals that the expression is being adopted in the early going. These examples will be important to lean on when the inevitable reviews and personal opinions of those who don't like it come flooding in. At AU, our giveaway of free t-shirts that proudly proclaimed what kind of wonk one was flooded the campus with 5,000 walking endorsements in the early days. At the AU Admissions Welcome Center and at major events, we gave away Wonk campaign buttons of all sorts in brand colors that looked like bowls full of candy; they proved irresistible to those who visited and wanted to brandish a token of the kind of wonk they were or hoped to be. A photo contest invited students to take and submit a selfie with their favorite wonk display ad; these ads were posted in the City of Washington in key locations targeting spring admission visitors, federal workers who were considering graduate degrees, alumni, and parents. We also established a World of Wonks website, where students, faculty, staff, and alumni could "check in" on a world map with a profile that included their wonk status. All along, we kept track of examples of departments, student organizations, and speakers using the brand expression in their work.

At the University of Maryland, after the launch of the "ZOOM" campaign, we were astonished to realize that the two leading candidates in the state's gubernatorial race were citing in their stump speeches facts from our television commercials as evidence of the university's rapid momentum and growing recognition of its quality. Capturing and documenting evidence of such adoption can be enormously helpful in reporting on the early impact of marketing efforts.

Karl Einolf, president of Indiana Tech, noted that internal audiences wanted to know right away about the impact of their new brand strategy—as expressed in the campaign "Go for IT" and leveraging their acronym, IT—especially given the expense. "I can see that it has made a considerable difference in the excitement that we have with traditional students. We recruited a great class for this fall, on the heels of the new strategy," he reported in 2019, "and that is only going to grow." In 2020, after his institution moved all in-person instruction online and directed all nonessential personnel to work remotely during the pandemic, Einolf reported that "we've been using our brand concept as part of a rallying cry for our community of students, faculty, coaches and staff to stay engaged with one another—we are in IT together, unity, etc. It's been fascinating to see how our students connect with this message, and I'm glad the brand was in place for 18 months before COVID-19 hit us."[12]

He reiterated the cautions of his marketing partner, Simpson-Scarborough, who advised that the internal community "will be sick of all the new stuff before it penetrates the market, so we need to be patient with it. Overall it has been well received and we will keep monitoring it going forward."[13] Einolf assures constituents who inquire that Indiana Tech will replicate aspects of the original study that formed the strategy and report on it to the community, continuing the transparent communication that leaders there have engaged in from the beginning of the process.

Leaders are advised not to make radical changes to strategy or expression unless the early indicators are overwhelmingly concerning or negative. There are a few notable examples, like the D+ campaign at Drake University, which simply could not be reasonably sustained, given the negative sentiment among key audiences. In most instances, however, if the strategy and expression were well formed, based on data, and tested prior to launch, the sentiment might be mixed, but early indicators will show that the messages are being recognized, pickup is happening, and evidence of adoption is promising. That is the basis for adjustment and sustainment of the effort.

Middle-Term Measures

Two to three years into the establishment or refreshment of a brand strategy, in addition to regular monitoring of proxy measures, it is reasonable to take stock of progress toward the goals of the strategy. Expectations should be modest. Because perceptions of an institution and its reputation change slowly over time, changes in awareness, familiarity, favorability, and preference will be incremental at best. If the institution is expanding to new markets, awareness and familiarity might even be lower overall among certain audiences, such as prospective students. However, if the measures show that the institution is gaining on competitors, overall and in markets where the institution is expanding, that's still important progress toward the long-term goal.

Ideally, the institution would want to replicate some or all of the research that formed the basis of the brand strategy. There might be new research questions that focus on recall or recognition of the key messages in the brand expression. Two and a half years after the "WONK" campaign was introduced at American, more than 90 percent of students, faculty, staff, and alumni recognized the campaign and could recall basic messages, for example; and as mentioned earlier, they were able to recall, without assistance or prompting, some of the key brand associations designed to help the university stand out among competitors.

But even in instances when the institution does not want to, or chooses not to, spend resources on replication of the original study in the first few years, there are other, less costly options for regularly testing awareness, familiarity, and favorability. Omnibus surveys of public opinion, which survey voters or consumers about a range of products, services, or industries, are an easy and inexpensive way to participate in research that the institution does not lead or own. Often, large advertising agencies or market research firms conduct such studies, charging an institution per item. In such a case, an institution would want to try to form survey questions similar to those in the original market research, focused on the goals of the strategy. The samples and respondents won't be exactly the same, so the results cannot be compared to demonstrate a clear and reliable difference in outcomes, but this measurement option is a good, less expensive alternative in the early years. Especially for public institutions, such surveys of voters and regional audiences can be a cost-effective means of tracking progress.

It is worth noting that not everything might be working at an optimal level. Signs that the expression is not registering in the early going, or that there are no changes on important proxy measures, or that there is no incremental change in the measures related to the overall strategy might be sufficient to warrant adjustments in the tactics or even in elements of the strategy. Institutions are advised not to make radical changes based on two or three years of data. Frequent changes in brand expression or strategy are at best confusing and at worst wasteful.

At the University of Maryland, two years after the launch of our first brand campaign, "ZOOM," many of the proxy measures were indicating progress in the right direction, but we were not yet prepared to invest in a replication of the study that had led to the formation of our brand strategy. However, we were already receiving feedback from internal audiences that they were tired of using the creative expression and wanted to know when we would change to something new. Indeed, the concept itself was a bit gimmicky, and the test that President Dan Mote liked to use—did it "have legs"?—seemed to suggest that it would not hold up over a long period of time, despite tweaks we could make. We chose to invest in development of a new expression, "Fear the Turtle," which was built on exactly the same brand platform and targeted the same strategic outcomes. That meant investment to develop recognition of the campaign and its messages, time and money that could have been saved had we stuck with the original expression. However, "Fear the Turtle" proved in the early going that it better met the requirements for a strong brand strategy and that it did indeed have legs. This is a good example of the decisions about adjustments and the balance that leaders must achieve when weighing alternatives.

Long-Term Measures

Throughout this chapter, emphasis has been placed on tracking and monitoring proxy measures, which are outcomes that should move in a positive direction if the strategy and expression are working effectively. In three years and beyond, outcomes associated with the behaviors of target audiences that reflect awareness, support, and loyalty should be better than at the start, and if they are not, it is time to consider an adjustment in expression, underlying strategy, or both. (Leaders who have arrived since the introduction of the brand strategy are well advised to understand the value that has been invested prior to their arrival and to consider the wisdom of building on that value for the greatest impact if it is showing results rather than starting anew for the sake of putting one's own mark on the brand.)

In addition, it is definitely time to replicate a study of the questions that formed the original strategy and relate directly to strategic goals. Sufficient time has passed, and it is reasonable to see measurable differences in awareness and familiarity, especially on the part of audiences in which there has been targeted investment. Favorability and perceptions of reputation can reasonably be expected to improve if they were targeted in the strategy and messages and if investments targeting the audiences were made.

Questions that target favorability, quality, or reputation come in many forms. If they were asked in a certain way in the original market research, there is great value in replication, because progress can be easily measured and reported. Types of questions include unaided awareness: "Name excellent universities in Los Angeles." They could be asked in the form of aided awareness, allowing ratings of the institution and specific competitors of interest on a Likert scale: "Rate the quality of academic programs at each of the following schools." Respondents can be asked to clarify which institutions are the very best: "In your opinion, which two of the following schools have the strongest image and reputation?" The frequency with which the institution is mentioned can be measured by audience and tracked over time.

Areas of inquiry that were mentioned among middle-term measures can be repeated, and deeper recognition and greater recall of messages and differentiation should be apparent. Respondents can also be queried about change in the reputation of the institution in the period since the strategy was implemented: "In the last three years, has the university's reputation gotten better, gotten worse, or stayed the same?" On this question, majorities of every American University stakeholder audience said the institution had gotten better, with 60 percent or more of current undergraduates, faculty, staff, alumni, and parents of current undergraduates saying the reputation had improved. Perceptions of graduate students and prospective students were less relevant on this question, primarily because these audiences had a shorter relationship with the institution (they arrived or connected within the three-year period in question).

Audiences can even be asked about the brand strategy and its expression. Examples of the creative work used to express the brand can be shown and the respondents asked, "Do these ads have a positive or negative impact on the institution's reputation, or no impact at all?" Majorities of every audience at American said the impact of the ads was positive.

If something significant has happened at the institution since the brand strategy was launched or refined, there may be a desire to explore the impact of the event or change. Perhaps a campus issue had wide media coverage and there are concerns about its impact on reputation. Perhaps as the college has proceeded in its strategic plan a potential new differentiator has emerged and the institution wants to test its relevance, authenticity, and distinctiveness with various audiences. This presents an opportunity to explore the value of a potential adjustment to the brand strategy or expression, just as in the original research when potential key positioning messages were tested.

A research professional or partner and the goals that formed the basis of the strategy should be the guides to inform the gathering of long-term measures so that there is confidence and relevance in both the method and analysis. If appreciable differences are not observed in the analysis of these measures, leaders should revisit not only the strategy and expression but the investment by audience. It is not reasonable to see changes among audiences who were not targeted with specific and sustained marketing tactics over the course of the period being measured. It could be that adjustments are necessary in the investment, either overall or in terms of allocation for specific audiences. I have always found better results when limited investments were focused like a laser on the primary audience of greatest strategic interest rather than sprinkled broadly, but not deeply, across many different audiences. The latter is a recipe for no change.

Regular Reporting

This chapter, and indeed this whole book, advocates a process that is participatory, transparent, and heavy on frequent communication, particularly with internal audiences. Buy-in and support for the investments are developed through regular reporting and adjustments along the way. Leaders may find ways to report on the effects of the strategy in annual reports, town hall meetings, cabinet meetings, board meetings, or other regular leadership communication. The institution's marketing task force should be the first audience for these reports, and the members can help to make meaning of results and be advocates of the work, just as they were at the initial stages of strategy formation. Reporting might be more frequent in the short term and revert to annual reporting as the strategy matures.

One caveat relates to how widely the results should be reported and distributed. Like the original strategy, the results will reflect competitive advantages and disadvantages. Therefore I have always treated them as proprietary. I don't believe in providing competitors with a playbook showing how we are beating them; just as firmly, I believe in keeping the campus community informed. Working with information technology partners, leaders can provide read-only documents on intranet sites or portals, and even then, what is provided in written form might be an edited summary, while detailed results can be shared confidentially with internal audiences in person.

Return on Investment

One last form of measurement worth mentioning, *return on investment*, or *ROI*, is a relative measure. If the data on marketing expenses and revenue generated are properly recorded and coded, ROI measures can be used to evaluate both specific tactics and overall brand strategy investments. The recording, coding, and gathering of such data are no small feat, especially at large and complex institutions, where authority and resources for this work are often widely distributed. Since this form of measurement is specifically designed to evaluate the value of investment, we will treat it in more detail in the next chapter.

> ### Key Questions for Leaders and Their CMOs
>
> - What are the expectations for our branding work in the short, middle, and long term?
>
> - What are the marketing and communication key performance indicators we could measure across university

units, and could we compile the data to identify useful insights?

- How regularly do we plan to conduct brand research?

- If our branding efforts are not producing the expected results, how will we refine and adjust?

Chapter 8

Marketing Investment and Return on Investment

It's not easy to track exactly how much institutions spend on marketing. . . . Different institutions include different things in their marketing budgets, making it difficult to pin down precisely what is spent where.

—Bob Brock, CEO, Education Marketing Group

Based on how quickly my conversations with presidents and other leaders turn to the expense of marketing, I'm guessing that many leaders will scan this chapter straight off the bat. No doubt, the investment in a strategic function that builds value will require significant investment up front, but it would be a mistake to see it only through the lens of expense. Indeed, the essential premise of this book is that effective marketing builds value. It should yield revenue and build reputational equity, which in turn motivates students to enroll and be retained through graduation, alumni and other donors to engage in philanthropy and advocacy, partners to become and remain engaged, and employees to be retained and proud.

Given the competitive climate and the demographic headwinds facing institutions, leaders have begun to see marketing as an essential strategic function that goes well beyond messaging to develop a differentiated position relative to competitor institutions and to communicate and deliver on the promises made. Nathan Grawe's dire enrollment projections for the second half of the next decade signaled that the time had come for institutions to build their marketing strategy and invest resources, before the sector faced the worst of the downturn in a few years' time.[1] The potentially devastating effects of the global pandemic and the resulting economic downturn (the magnitude of which has yet to be fully understood as I write this) may have shortened the time to prepare for the demographic cliff or perhaps hastened its arrival. Investments in strategic integrated marketing may be more essential than ever to institutional survival.

In this chapter, we review trends and provide the most detailed guidance available on current investment in marketing by institutional type, provide counsel on the source of funds, and explore how to set up and measure return on investment (ROI) through relevant metrics.

Funding a Successful Marketing Program

Presidents are often concerned with and challenged to determine the level of resources to apply to the work of marketing and branding the institution, especially relative to other funding priorities. Presidents who have come up through the faculty ranks are likely to be concerned about both the optics and the real trade-offs between investments in marketing and those that build faculty, academic facilities, research centers, and academic programs.

Neil Kerwin, president emeritus at American University, privately acknowledged early in our work together at American University that he was working to overcome an academic bias against marketing that he had held for most of his career. Nevertheless, he made a deliberate choice to include the goals of marketing as an explicit part of the strategic plan (expressed in language that academic colleagues would find acceptable, related to winning recognition and distinction) and supported investments that represented about 1 percent of the total annual budget. In

2009, that stood out as a relatively large investment for a non-profit environment, and that led to an imperative to demonstrate *return on investment*. Kerwin insisted on documenting the work and demonstrating results, including standards of measurement for everything in which we invested. We used pilots that expanded if we showed results and sunset if we didn't, experimented with appropriate ROI metrics, and established regular periodic surveys of stakeholder perceptions to track our progress until the impact could be felt and recognized by stakeholders. We established a foundation for proving that the resources invested benefitted the institution in ways that had an important influence on enrollment and reputation.

The data for benchmarking investments in marketing are limited for several reasons. First, it is difficult to collect data on expenditures when marketing responsibilities and resources are distributed so widely on many campuses. Second, there is no normative organizational structure to direct what capacities and comparable expenses should be included in any calculation of the investment. Third, those who are inclined to provide such data may not identify whether the expenditures include operating budgets, salaries, benefits, or all three. Wide variances are reflected in the few sources we have available.

For a 2019 feature on the marketing function at Southern New Hampshire University, *Inside Higher Ed* spoke to Bob Brock, CEO of Educational Marketing Group (EMG), an agency that tracks spending on higher education marketing. "'It's not easy to track exactly how much institutions spend on marketing. . . . Different institutions include different things in their marketing budgets, making it difficult to pin down precisely what is spent where.' Comparing marketing budgets across different institutions is also difficult for that reason, but Brock estimates that the average private nonprofit spends under 5 percent of its annual revenue on marketing."[2]

Though leaders may find the available data confounding at times, I find it hopeful that we are at least beginning to estimate and explore options for benchmarking, with perhaps more precision becoming available in the future. What is currently known about higher education marketing expenditures is presented here. Leaders are encouraged to be guided by it in the context of their own institutions as they consider investments and expectations for return.

Average Marketing Expenditures by Institutional Type

One source of data on marketing investment comes from the previously mentioned survey of CMOs at nonprofit four-year institutions conducted by SimpsonScarborough. The 2014 and 2019 iterations gathered data about marketing expenditures. Appropriate caution should be taken in interpreting the report of expenditures, since it cannot be determined exactly what resources were reported in the calculation of salaries and operating expenses. That is, it is not clear whether the calculations include resources for the central marketing unit alone or also include resources for distributed marketing units. Nor is it clear which marketing capacities were funded in these units.

While acknowledging these limits, in 2014 we got a useful first look at average dollar expenditures annually at different types of institutions (table 3). Average dollar expenditures ranged from $1.3 million to $3.6 million annually. The extremes at both the high and the low end are very much outliers, creating great variance between the mean and median expenditures for each institutional type.

In 2019, average dollar expenditures ranged from $1.1 million to $3.4 million annually (table 4). These average budgets show little change from the first survey. Indeed, in 2019 roughly half of the respondents said their budgets had remained the same as in the previous year; more than a quarter said theirs had increased; and nearly a quarter said theirs had decreased. Reflecting the complexity of marketing organizational structures and the widely distributed responsibilities and funding, 20 percent

TABLE 3. *Annual marketing expenditures at four-year nonprofit institutions by type, 2014*

| | Type of Institution | | |
Annual expenditure	Doctoral	Master's	Baccalaureate
Mean	$3,559,111	$2,271,863	$1,259,893
Median	2,800,000	1,400,000	1,000,000
Minimum	300,000	200,000	100,000
Maximum	25,000,000	18,000,000	7,000,000

Source: Adapted from Chronicle Insights Group, "Higher Ed Marketing Comes of Age: Data and Insights from College Marketing Leaders" (Washington, DC: Chronicle of Higher Education, 2014), http://results.chronicle.com/CMOAMA.

TABLE 4. *Annual marketing expenditures at four-year nonprofit institutions by type, 2019*

| | Type of Institution | | |
Annual expenditure	Doctoral	Master's	Baccalaureate
Mean	$3,379,074	$1,730,611	$1,126,287
Median	2,500,000	1,600,000	1,000,000
Minimum	455,800	300,000	150,000
Maximum	12,000,000	2,000,000	3,700,000
% of CMOs unable to supply data	15%	21%	20%

Source: Adapted from SimpsonScarborough, "The 2019 State of Higher Ed Marketing," 2019, simpsonscarborough.com/CMOStudy, 15.

of CMOs could not estimate the annual marketing budgets at their own institutions.

Percentage of Annual Budget

The percentage of the annual budget as a benchmark for marketing investment comes from the corporate world. When I started out in higher education marketing in the late nineties, the corporate sector was dedicating 3-5 percent of the annual budget to marketing; by 2019 that percentage had doubled.[3] In my experience, very few nonprofit institutions have reached an investment of 10 percent or greater, and there have been wide fluctuations within and across sectors, not at all like what we are seeing in terms of digital marketing and recruitment for online programs, which have recently been documented as being as high as 19 percent of tuition revenue.[4]

In the 2019 survey, for the first-time budgets were reported in terms of percentage of annual budget. CMOs at nonprofit four-year institutions who could estimate and report their total annual marketing budget had an average (mean) percentage of total institutional budget for marketing ranging from 1.39 percent for doctoral institutions, to 2.00 percent for master's institutions, and 2.93 percent for baccalaureate institutions. (The extremes include minimums of less than 1% for all three types of institutions and maximums ranging from 9.06% to 15%.)[5] A large majority (78%) of these CMOs did not agree that they had sufficient resources to meet the expectations of their leadership.[6] That is understandable, given the average marketing budget as a percentage of institutional total budget.

An annual American Marketing Association survey of CMOs shows that spending varies widely by industry and that the education sector, broadly speaking, has an average total marketing spend, including salaries and operating expenditures, of 11 percent.[7] This is likely influenced in part by for-profits, OPMs, and others invested in large-scale online education. For example, 2U revealed that it spends closer to 19 percent, and the nonprofit online behemoth Southern New Hampshire University spends 17 percent of annual revenues on marketing.[8]

For start-ups and small businesses, the benchmark is closer to 1-3 percent, which might be a good comparison for colleges and universities just beginning to engage in significant marketing efforts. Just as it would be difficult for a new business to commit to the average percentage for its sector, it would be impractical for an institution just starting to increase its investment in marketing to go from a negligible amount to 5-10 percent in one budget cycle.

In my own work in consultation with a small, private liberal arts colleges building their marketing organization and investment, I demonstrated that comparable institutions were investing 3.5-4 percent of their total annual budget in 2019. I had a chance to review the marketing expenditures for two small private colleges. One, already engaged in significant branding and enrollment, had a total marketing budget equal to 4 percent annually. The other's was just under 3 percent, but as it prepared to engage in repositioning, it expected to increase that investment. For comparison purposes, I was able to anonymously review the repositioning investments of four small colleges and universities that had engaged an agency for help in branding. Two were public and two were private, with enrollments ranging from 1,600 to 8,700. While I was unable to ascertain the marketing expenditures as a percentage of the annual budget, I was able to learn that their total investment for the first year of brand development and implementation for enrollment marketing ranged between $800,000 and $1.2 million, which aligns closely with the median annual budget of $1 million for baccalaureate colleges in the 2014 and 2019 CMO studies.[9] I was also able to learn how the funds were allocated. Roughly 20-25 percent of the total was spent on the initial repositioning (research and recommendations). Another quarter was spent on fees for strategy and creative development, and the balance, roughly half, was spent on media (costs to develop and place the brand ads in various paid media channels). Larger institutions, with more constituents and larger budgets, and institutions in expensive media markets would reasonably expect the investment total to be higher, but the marketing expenditure (4% of total annual budget) and the proportional aspects of the initial agency investment are instructive.

Institutions looking to establish a brand in new markets or to reposition themselves usually need to increase resource investments to register awareness and achieve greater engagement. The total annual investment may decrease over time, since the strategy development is complete, but the maintenance of the effort through paid media should remain constant, at least for a few years. For an institution with a mature brand position, media costs might ramp down slightly. However, it is worth noting that with so much of the work now happening in the digital environment, costs for developing and placing paid media have increased (largely a function of the number of targeted pieces that must be produced, placed, and tracked in the online environment). Moreover, constant attention on SEO strategies to establish and maintain organic search position requires significant staff or agency time.

Relationship of Marketing Budget to Marketing Effectiveness

The 2019 survey also asked CMOs to rate the effectiveness of their own institutions' overall marketing efforts over the last three years, using letter grades, and presented the results in terms of marketing effectiveness. The results were categorized by the institutions' marketing budget per student (using full-time equivalents, or FTEs). Those awarding their institution an A reported markedly better results in terms of enrollment, annual fundraising, and reputation gains than those who gave their institutional efforts a C or D. Twenty-one percent of CMOs gave their institutions an A, and their annual total marketing budget per student averaged $623. The majority (59%) gave their institutions a B, and their total marketing budget per student averaged $429. Another 29 percent gave their institutions a C or D for marketing effectiveness, and their total marketing budget per student averaged $463.[10] The report of this CMO survey did not analyze marketing budget per student by institutional type, but in the future this could be a comparative benchmark worth reporting and tracking.

Public Media Coverage of Marketing Spending

Recent media coverage of online juggernauts is beginning to improve comparative data and trends related to marketing investment. The 2019 *Inside Higher Ed* report on Southern New Hampshire University—one of the largest nonprofit institutions in the United States, with 132,000 students, most of them online—focused on its marketing practices and budget. Digital marketing and advertising investments have propelled SNHU's success, with annual marketing expenditures of $139 million and a nearly equal annual net surplus of $133 million.[11]

"Twenty sixteen was the first time in history that private nonprofit expenditures exceeded those of for-profits," according to Brock of EMG, who said the for-profits spent $607.7 million on marketing in 2016, while private nonprofits spent $611 million.[12] In recent years, for-profit institutions have faced regulatory, shareholder, and enrollment challenges and reined in marketing spending (relatively speaking), while the marketing expenditures at private nonprofits, many building online programs and adopting digital marketing practices, or the first time exceeded those at for-profit institutions.

While the SNHU expenditures are eye-popping compared with those of most nonprofit institutions, so are the returns, and the proportional expenditures for digital marketing and media buying are instructive for leaders thinking about the allocation of resources. SNHU's most recent tax filing shows that 34 percent of its annual marketing expenditures went to Google for digital marketing, and 61 percent went to the institution's media buying and planning agency. Other categories of marketing expenditures included market research, website operations, communication with current students, social media, student experience, signage on campus, employee communication, and video and creative teams.[13]

Brock rated SNHU's marketing as highly effective and notes the relationship between quality efforts and ROI. "They are likely seeing a very good return on investment," he said. "They produce A-plus-quality materials, which is important, because audiences today are sophisticated consumers. We've all seen millions of ads and can judge really quickly if someone put in the effort or tried to do something cheap."[14]

On the basis of these reports, what can leaders conclude about the right level of funding for strategic marketing initiatives? Certainly that the average investment at most institutions is not sufficient to meet leaders' expectations; that the average investment for the education sector as a whole, 11 percent, is politically unrealistic for most nonprofit institutions that have not previously invested in marketing and demonstrated that the process yields value; that institutions reporting the best results related to marketing goals have higher investments than those reporting poor outcomes; and that it is possible to develop a return on investment that builds revenue, as well as reputation, over and above the original investment.

While weighing the optics of investing in marketing and seeking comparative investment data in higher education or other sectors, savvy leaders realize that sufficiency of resources must be determined by the marketing goals to be achieved. A major repositioning strategy for an institution with a century or more of history or an institution seeking to expand to new markets that are unfamiliar with it will require more resources to meet its goals than an institution that is seeking to maintain its brand or extend relationships with stakeholders from basic awareness to deeper engagement and loyalty. As leaders seek to better understand their institution's market position vis-à-vis its competitors and to develop marketing strategies to build or leverage a strong market position, they can better estimate the financial and human resources needed to implement the strategy.

I would advise leaders who want to invest in this process to build value that they should plan to work toward an investment of 3–5 percent of total budget, depending on the marketing goals and strategic outcomes the investments are intended to achieve.

Measure results assiduously and increase investments to yield greater returns when the results warrant.

Sources of Funds

Institutional control influences decisions related to sources of funds for marketing and advertising. While public and private institutions historically invest dollars in admissions and recruitment, when it comes to expenditures categorized as marketing or advertising, often seen solely as "promotion," there is great sensitivity about using taxpayer dollars for this purpose. At the University of Maryland, our first brand campaigns were funded with private funds raised by and allocated from the university's foundation. Such an approach might be particularly important for public institutions just starting to raise their investments in these areas, at least until their impact is clearly demonstrated.

Board members' expertise on the resources required and their political support are invaluable, but they may also play a unique role in terms of investment: they may be motivated to support marketing with use of private funds or to personally contribute. At public institutions, in particular, their philanthropic support or encouragement of other donors can fund marketing efforts when use of public dollars and tuition are not a smart political option. Foundation funds at the University of Maryland provided support for a new university visual identity program (logo system) and its first branding campaign. One trustee, Robert Facchina, was so inspired by the impact of the "Fear the Turtle" campaign that he provided the blank canvas of several 18-wheel trucks—which carried yogurt and other dairy products from his company, Johanna Foods, up and down I-95 every day—to carry brand advertising as a gift in kind (fig. 5).

Even private institutions face pressure regarding use of tuition dollars, which are the primary source of revenue for the vast majority of tuition-dependent institutions. Scrutiny of expenditures has increased along with tuition rates, and institu-

Figure 5. University of Maryland "Fear the Turtle" campaign ads on display at the university's sesquicentennial celebration in Baltimore, Maryland, 2006. Several 18-wheel delivery trucks traveling I-95 daily were wrapped with these ads, donated as a gift in kind by Johanna Foods, whose CEO served on the university's foundation board. Courtesy of University of Maryland.

tions that need to justify or defend marketing expenditures are wise to do so transparently, framing marketing as more than mere promotion. As with any other important strategic function, it takes time and money to yield high-quality marketing results. As a strategic function that builds value, investments should be presented as both strategic expenditures and in the context of the return on investment.

Return on Investment

There are literally dozens of measures of ROI in the corporate sector. By way of example, a couple of simple measures will provide data on the relative value and productivity of various higher education marketing investments. However, gathering the data and developing the capacity to analyze them requires significant effort.

Cost of Acquisition

At the most basic level, cost of acquisition is an easy and important measure for reviewing overall return and relative effectiveness and performance. If an institution properly codes, tracks, and collects data on expenditures that reflect marketing expenditures, and does so consistently across units and from year to year, a simple calculation of marketing expenditures per student will provide a relative measure of performance. The metric can be used to zero in on expenditures divided by inquiries, expenditures divided by applicants, and expenditures divided by enrolled students. A declining cost of student acquisition year to year reflects more productive efforts and, by definition, greater revenue. Such a metric also allows institutions to determine which markets have the lowest cost of acquisition, which they can use to adapt their enrollment strategy.

Lifetime Value

In the previous chapter, on measures, Robert Moore and Tom Abrahamson's concept of lifetime value of a student or alumnus was introduced.[15] This is another relative measure. It is an estimate derived from institutional data to help institutions hone their enrollment and fundraising strategies and measure the related marketing investments, putting them in the context of other long-term investment alternatives (endowments, real estate, etc.).

Calculating ROI

The challenge of calculating an actual return on investment requires a level of precision that is neither practical nor cost-effective for most institutions. It would require that data be held or derived in terms of net revenue for every student enrolled, every alumna's gift (after subtracting the costs associated with cultivation, stewardship, and administration associated with executing the gift agreement), every dollar spent on marketing, and data on results of those investments, directly tying them to the enrollment or gift. However, it is possible to derive a close approximation of actual net revenue if expenditures are properly tracked, coded, and collected. Even then, to do so will require a partnership between the CMO, the CFO, and provost or chief academic officer.

At American University, we piloted a framework for ROI by enlisting the support of my cabinet colleagues. First, I enlisted the support of the provost to help me persuade the deans and their marketing staff members to supply data on their marketing expenditures. This might sound easy, but it was politically sensitive. As in many universities, the authority and responsibility for marketing expenditures was distributed across the colleges and schools. Especially for units following a responsibility-centered management model, such a request was perceived to be intrusive. Some deans and their teams were not keen to share the details of their expenditures, nor to participate in something they feared would expose wasteful efforts. Others were not anxious to compare outcomes across units. Of course, the CFO could have extracted data at an institutional level without their cooperation, but the level of detail about expenditures and the danger of uniformed assumptions made the prospect less than optimal, and it would not have built cooperation and trust around a process designed to build and enhance value—something every leader needs. Instead, the provost and I sought to work with the deans to provide the rationale for such an endeavor, highlighting the benefits of such an experiment and assuring them that we would not use the results of the pilot to diminish or take away resources. Any outcomes would be shared, with analysis provided at the unit and institutional levels so that leaders could use the information as they saw fit.

Having secured the participation and cooperation of the deans, we worked with their marketing directors to extract and understand their data on marketing expenditures. We found and had to address hurdles such as differences in budget codes used to categorize expenses, as well as expenditures that straddled more than one fiscal year. In addition, we needed to tie enrollment data to inquiries and prospects going back at least two years (because many students take more than one year to proceed from consideration to application and enrollment). This task is more easily surmounted if an enterprise-wide CRM exists to track the data. If there is no CRM, or if there is more than one on a campus, then lists with information that can identify and track enrolling students to their inquiry information must be preserved. At American, we collectively made decisions about how to consistently track and count the data so that in future years we would have consistent and comparable results.

Next, we worked with the CFO's budget director and a business analyst to develop the information on finances and enrollment. Together, we developed a model that revealed ROI measures such as net revenue and cost of acquisition for our key enrollment segments. The work wasn't without challenges or compromises, but together we successfully reviewed several years of marketing investments and returns. For specific formulas to develop the ROI calculations, I commend Moore and Abrahamson, who have written the seminal work for higher education ROI.

Tracking the finances and outcomes data (e.g., enrollment or fundraising) must be done cycle by cycle, and week by week, in order to generate the ROI. Using enrollment as an example, Moore and Abrahamson suggest that an institution will need to track prospects, inquiries, campus visits, applicants, stealth applicants, enrollment, and discount rate for new first-year students for each term and similarly, inquiries, applicants, and total enrolled (FTE) transfer and graduate students.[16] Then, an institution will need to track total revenue from tuition and fees, revenue per segment (first-year, transfer, graduate), and marketing spend. Using these data, ROI is derived from the following equation:

$$\text{ROI} = (\text{Gain from Investment} - \text{Cost of Investment}) / \text{Cost of Investment}$$

As Moore and Abrahamson point out, it sounds simple, but it isn't. In addition to the administrative and political hurdles noted, there is the matter of backing out fixed costs. Instead, the authors suggest an incremental ROI, which suggests establishing an institution's historical marketing budget and then developing the enhanced ROI, which calculates the incremental cost and return of every strategy and tactic that is added to the existing or standard marketing spend:

$$\text{ROI\%} = (\text{Incremental Benefits} - \text{Incremental Costs}) / \text{Incremental Costs} \times 100$$

The authors remind users, "Success is not measured tactic by tactic, though in order to manage the eventual outcome you have to track with that level of specificity. The overall measure of success will be the increased revenue delivered by all the strategies and tactics combined, and if you adjust as the campaign moves forward, to put more support behind those activities that are return the greatest result, your net effect will be better."[17]

Data Analyst Support

Another lesson learned about experimenting with a means to track and measure ROI is that the heightened need for data and analysis will likely require professional expertise that may not be in the marketing shop. Hence the need for data analysts and business intelligence specialists who are dedicated to this work full time. CMOs and presidents might consider a position dedicated to the tracking analysis that works in the marketing department, or they might consider whether the expertise exists elsewhere at the institution and can be reallocated to this task.

Brand Equity

Another measure of marketing effectiveness that relates to investment exists in other sectors but hasn't yet been successfully established in higher education. The *Oxford English Dictionary* defines *brand equity* as the commercial value that derives from consumer perception of the brand name of a particular product or service, rather than from the product or service itself. It relates to the measurement of the value of a brand over and above the value of the product or service, or the premium that is derived from a respected name compared with a generic equivalent.[18] Brand equity provides value not only to organizations but also to customers, whose ability to process and interpret information is enhanced, and whose confidence in their purchase decisions and user experience are enhanced by strong brands.[19] The change in brand equity over time is a measure of change in reputational value.

Since higher education is not very good at establishing the cost of education or of measuring and communicating the value, it makes sense that it would be difficult to measure the added value of the brand. But we are already learning to track elements of brand equity, such as brand awareness and loyalty, brand associations and perceived quality. Look for measures of higher education brand equity to emerge in the future as the profession continues to mature and develop. It is a natural extension of the view that marketing builds value in terms of both revenue and reputation.

Establishing Expectations

I recognize how hard it is to consider a major investment in marketing, especially if the historical investments have been small relative to other measures. However, any strategic function that builds value requires an upfront investment. In the context of other institutional investments, the decision about whether to invest in marketing is no different than decisions about investments in recruitment, fundraising, endowment management, real estate, and facilities. It will take time, money, and professional expertise to produce the desired results. A frank conversation should be had between the CMO, the president, and cabinet colleagues about what strategic goals are to be influenced by marketing and what measures will be used to track effectiveness. The board will likely need to approve expenditures at the levels addressed in this chapter; if so, trustees are likely to be influenced by a commitment to track, measure, and adjust based on outcomes.

Knowing what we know is coming in the next decade, institutions are well advised to start planning, investing, measuring, and reporting on marketing investments so that the most effective strategies begin to mature before the demographic "cliff" hits with full force.

Key Questions for Leaders and Their CMOs

- What percentage of the overall university operating budget does marketing and communication represent? If we don't know, can the provost and CFO help us gather that information?

- What should be the sources of funds for our marketing investments?

- If we invest more in marketing and communication, what results can we expect, and in what time frame?

Chapter 9

The Future of Higher Education Marketing

We are flying blind into a dangerous period for higher education.
  —Nathan Grawe, author and professor of economics, Carleton College

Fifteen years ago, it was impossible to utter the M-word on a college campus without experiencing disdain for commercial and business practices that many thought were antithetical to an academic institution. It would have been hard to imagine then the extent to which attitudes would change and marketing leadership, practices, and systems would be introduced on college and university campuses, if not fully embraced or matured at the level of sophistication seen in other industry sectors. Rapid developments in technology and communication have changed the practice of marketing even as we have been learning how to adapt in the context of higher education.

Is it possible to anticipate what the next 15 years will hold? The impact of the global health and economic crisis introduced by the COVID-19 pandemic is yet to be fully understood but likely will be felt for years to come, and that has made anticipating even the next few years a murky proposition. Undoubtedly, the crisis provides opportunities to innovate and rethink overall institutional strategy, including opportunities to explore new markets, consider elements of the marketing mix, and even to significantly reposition an institution. This chapter focuses on trends that leaders should carefully track as they consider how to build and maintain relevant and effective strategic marketing efforts.

Higher education marketing efforts over the next decade and a half will surely be shaped by two strong forces expected to radically disrupt the sector: the dramatic projected declines in college-aged and college-going populations in the United States and the changes in the future of work—indeed in most forms of employment—as a result of technological advances in artificial intelligence and machine learning. The first force is likely to further underscore the importance of marketing as a strategic function that is critical to building value, and the second is likely to radically change the way marketing is practiced.

The Impact of the Demographic Cliff

As Nathan Grawe points out, "We are flying blind into a dangerous period for higher education. Yet ten years before the brunt of the current birth dearth is abruptly felt in admissions offices across the country, we still lack demand forecasts that treat selective, national schools as distinct from the local community college. Decisions in the next five years will be critical in determining whether institutions thrive or flounder."[1]

The demographic declines are expected to hit the Northeast and the eastern Midwest particularly hard. Elite institutions are expected to thrive, though many will necessarily have to adjust their prime target markets, going deeper into current markets and expanding to new ones. That in turn will affect the prospects for other types of institutions. Two-year colleges are expected to be severely affected, and other four-year institutions more or less so, depending on their locations and the primary markets from which they draw. (This projection could change at least in the short term if students are inclined to stay closer to home or seek lower cost alternatives in the face of the global pandemic and recession.) Some areas of the South and the West are expected to see robust growth. Since most institutions will likely attempt to shift their recruitment attention to these areas of growth, the competition will be fierce, and as Grawe suggests, leaders should not be looking for financial relief from falling discount rates.[2] Indeed, competition for full-pay students will be even more fierce than it is today.

Since demand for new students is expected to decline, leaders should anticipate focus to shift to greater retention of enrolled students. Compounding the enrollment pressure introduced by the demographic decline, the impact of the pandemic on air travel and students' willingness to attend an institution far from home may make it harder to retain current students who come from greater distances. In addition, recent changes in admission practices that allow institutions to aggressively recruit students enrolled at other institutions may mean that retaining students will be more challenging than it has ever been.[3] For all of these reasons, the experience of existing customers will hold greater, perhaps even existential importance. Grawe suggests that higher education leaders make the most of their response to the pandemic, using what we have learned to bolster student success and retention efforts for student populations that were already changing dramatically.[4] Binding students to the institution through communication, engagement, and satisfying student experiences will be critical. In response to these anticipated challenges, the expertise of a strong CMO and marketing team will be more important than ever before.

The Role of the CMO

CMOs will be equipped in this environment to glean and use data to identify promising new target markets, develop institutional strategies that differentiate their institution from competitors, identify drivers of satisfaction and retention, personalize offers and communication, and ensure that programs, services, and experiences align with the brand promise. The increasing prominence of marketing as a strategic function that builds value is likely to encourage more leaders, even at the largest and most complex institutions, to make the CMO a member of the executive team.

The application of marketing tools, systems, and thinking to the challenges of student retention, employee satisfaction, donor retention, and alumni engagement may increase the development of CMOs as chief experience officers (CXOs), whose area of responsibility will increase in breadth, a trend that has already influenced other service sectors, such as health care. Institutions will have to wrestle with silos and barriers to integrated, relevant, and personalized experiences (in person and online), rooted in separate structures and reinforced in fractured technology platforms. As the importance of enterprise marketing technology, or *martech*, gives institutions a competitive advantage, CMOs will be well positioned to lead efforts that use data to understand the needs of specific segments and evaluate the effectiveness of strategies, use CRMs to cultivate and manage satisfying relationships, and use content strategy to deliver the right information at the right time. As the scope of CMO responsibility increases, leaders may consider greater investment in marketing as a percentage of overall budget and will expect clearer metrics of success and demonstrated return on investment.

The Future of Work

Artificial intelligence and machine learning are rapidly changing the nature of work and the types of employment in virtually every sector of the economy, as repetitive processes are being replaced with robotic automation and decision-making processes are being replaced with intelligent automation. These shifts will not only affect what kinds of education and workforce preparation colleges and universities offer; they will also influence how the work of providing education and services is done.

Opportunities for Differentiation

Joseph Aoun, president of Northeastern University, anticipates that college graduates will need skills in communication, creativity, collaboration, and complex thinking to compete in the twenty-first-century workforce, for positions that robots cannot assume.[5] Institutions that consider how to build and communicate strategies designed to focus on such competencies may have greater opportunities to differentiate in the coming competitive environment. With all due respect to Dr. Aoun, liberal arts institutions in particular would seem to have the inside track on developing such student outcomes if they can find ways to deliver and communicate their offerings in relevant and compelling ways. Brand research in the hands of marketing professionals would allow institutions to develop, test, and introduce such strategies before the worst of the enrollment contraction hits.

Impact on the Higher Education Marketing Workforce

A recent survey of CMOs in corporate environments revealed that most expect an increase in AI technologies to replace some of the work being done by employees in the next three years, "especially for companies that do a greater share of sales on the Internet."[6] If higher education follows past patterns, it will adopt more digital marketing practices that began in the corporate sector, albeit at a slower pace, including content personalization, development of customer insights, and targeting decisions, and these will be increasingly done through AI, which could replace not only marketing employees but perhaps also recruitment and admission staffers. This may be especially true for online programs, where digital marketing practices are standard. However, institutions that have adopted marketing technologies at an enterprise level, such as CMS, CRM, and marketing automation software, will be in the best position to enjoy the benefits of such technology advances and workforce efficiencies. Those that haven't adopted or integrated such tools at an enterprise level could lag further behind in terms of responsiveness, satisfaction, and service at a time when CMOs also expect customers to place a greater emphasis on excellent service and quality.[7]

Increasing Importance of Data and Analytics

Data to inform decisions about target markets, differentiated brand position, and student and alumni experience will be at more of a premium in the coming environment than it is today. Colleges and universities are swimming in data that are often unstructured or inaccessible at an enterprise level. But a strong CMO and digital team, working with the CIO and digital and business intelligence analysts, could unlock critical insights that allow institutions to outperform competitors in a resource-constrained environment. Data that inform institutional strategy, including brand strategy, should be an important foundation of strategic planning. Analytics gleaned from institutional websites and enterprise technology platforms should provide real-time and periodic performance measures that inform timely adjustments.

Governance around Content Strategy

It is unlikely that the ability to build a compelling narrative about an institution's distinct position will become less important in the context of the landscape looming on the horizon. But it may become even more important to deploy powerful, timely content in the form of personalized and targeted information to influence decisions about enrollment, retention, and satisfaction among stakeholders. CRMs and marketing automation tools make it possible to target and schedule content delivery if the content is structured in a format that meets stakeholder needs and expectations. Ironically, although universities are fountains of content, given our missions to discover and transmit knowledge, most content is not structured in a form that is ready to deploy in processes that will build value. Research papers and lectures don't grab eyeballs and ears the way videos and podcasts do. Devoting resources to the development of content strategy and the transformation of content resources to formats that will captivate, engage, and persuade stakeholders may become more crucial than ever.

Related to this, the development of voice-activated AI assistants that power search, manage schedules, operate home appliances, and start our vehicles is elevating the importance of audio content on organizational websites. However, very few institutions are currently focused on putting content in audio formats or in forms that screen readers can easily access through search. If there is a lesson from Mobilegeddon—the update made to Google's algorithm to elevate mobile-friendly content in search results in 2015—it is that institutions should be monitoring and planning for evolving trends in content format enabled by new technology. Many institutions were caught flat-footed with content that did not render on mobile devices even though the trend was identified by Educause and many others for years in advance of the shift. As a result, some institutions lost their high position in search results and had to scramble to put their web content in mobile-friendly formats. Similarly, institutions were well aware of developments that made content more assessible to those with visual, audio, and sensory disabilities, but many did not follow trend spotters' counsel to move toward the international accessibility standard (WCAG 2.0 AA) before shifts in US federal policy in 2017 put them at risk of noncompliance with updates to the Americans with Disabilities Act.[8] The lesson from both shifts is that technology makes it possible to access content in innovative ways, and institutions that monitor and adapt to such changes will possess a competitive advantage and avoid risk.

Innovations in Marketing and Business Strategy

Technological innovations enable or mandate changes in the way institutions market themselves, but they also offer opportunities to change the business strategy entirely. A trend worth watching in other sectors is platform strategy, which enables an organization or institution to enter a market by building a platform that allows participants to benefit from the presence of others.[9] Platforms like Facebook and Amazon make it possible for providers of goods and services to build their businesses by plugging into their platforms, as long as they meet a set of accepted standards. The aggregation of many users makes a platform attractive for businesses, and in turn, the presence of many products or services makes a platform attractive to many users. Institutions with scale may be in the best position to build a higher education platform with such potential, and arguably, edX and Coursera have tried. But could institutions the size of SNHU, Western Governor's University, or Arizona State University develop such a scale, and how might others find value in participating in such a platform? On platforms such as Uber, Lyft, and Airbnb, users in a sharing economy meet one another's needs. Passengers find drivers, and drivers find passengers. Those seeking short-term accommodations find those with the capacity to provide those accommodations. Is there a platform strategy embedded in the sharing economy that could disrupt the traditional higher education model, and what would that look like? What other disruptions in the business models in other sectors provide higher education with a new way to deliver or access their programs and services (the often neglected fourth P—or place—in the marketing mix)?

Improvements in Benchmarking of Investment and Performance

As the strategic function of marketing becomes more important, there will be greater pressure to collect and report comparative data on benchmarks of investment and performance that will allow leaders to make better decisions and achieve greater accountability for the results they aim to achieve and for return on the investments they make. Organizations like CASE and the AMA may play an important role in the development of such benchmarks and standards, and institutions will benefit from being able to assess outcomes relative to peer institutions and competitors. Institutions and agencies may also play an important role in innovations that lead to reliable and useful measurement of ROI and brand equity, as well as establishment of dashboards with short-, middle-, and long-term measures of brand performance.

In Conclusion

The future of marketing in higher education is informed by the past and the present. This book traces the development of higher education marketing as a strategic function that has matured and grown in sophistication, led by professionals whose expertise and counsel provide leaders with opportunities to build value in the form of revenue and reputation. The organizational structures of colleges and universities have naturally tended to diffuse the responsibility and authority of marketing leaders, but in recent years the role of CMOs on executive teams, their direct reporting to their presidents, and their effective use of both formal and informal power has elevated their influence and effectiveness.

Leaders' increasing recognition that institutional and brand strategies are parts of a greater whole allows institutions to realize the full potential of the marketing mix, including decisions about programs, price, and distribution strategies, rather than limiting the marketing function to primarily promotional decisions and activity. Leaders' understanding that strategic investment in marketing can build value across the enterprise may increase their willingness to increase investment as a percentage of total budget, more in line with other sectors and industries.

The use of data and digital tools has made the work more complex, but it has also opened new opportunities to target and personalize interactions with stakeholders for greater satisfaction, something that will be more critical as recruitment of new students and retention of current students becomes more challenging. As in the past, the cost of keeping and satisfying a current student or donor will likely be less than the cost of acquiring a new student or donor, and the return from retention therefore greater.

The role of research as the basis of marketing strategy and the foundation for measuring outcomes has made higher education marketing an institutional function guided by data and discipline. Measurement of inputs and outputs, especially return on investment, will be crucial for building confidence in the value of marketing and for increasing the CMO's accountability. Maturation of measures will allow greater opportunities to benchmark against peers or institutional comparators on investment, outcomes, and return.

Indeed, higher education marketing has come of age, and just in time. Leaders will face tremendous demographic headwinds in the decade ahead, while also finding little relief from the decline in public trust. Poor perceptions of the value of higher education, in part because of increasing cost and student debt, have been compounded by doubt about employment outcomes for graduates following the Great Recession and uncertainty about the changing nature of work. The global pandemic and its likely economic impact will heighten the financial stress many institutions were already experiencing, creating heightened enrollment marketing expectations and new opportunities.

Given these conditions, it is reasonable to speculate that marketing as a strategic function will only grow in importance and influence. Institutions that choose strategic differentiation, identify new target markets that align well with their differentiated position, shape satisfying experiences for students, alumni, and employees, measure and communicate the value of degrees and outcomes for graduates, and refine their strategy based on measurements that include return on investment will fare better in the climate ahead.

In short, not only has a strategic function that builds value come of age but higher education marketing may be entering a golden age of opportunity to help institutions survive and thrive.

Key Questions for Leaders and Their CMOs

- Do we expect the role of marketing and communication to become more or less important at our institution over the next five decades?

- Are we laying the groundwork for the expected shift?

Notes

Introduction. Why Marketing?

1. Jeffrey Jones, "Confidence in Higher Education Down Since 2015," *Gallup* (blog), October 9, 2018, https://news.gallup.com/opinion/gallup /242441/confidence-higher-education-down-2015.aspx?.

2. Jeffrey Selingo, "What Presidents Think: A 2013 Survey of Four-Year College Presidents," *Chronicle of Higher Education*, 2013, https://www .maguireassoc.com/wp-content/uploads/2015/08/Chronicle-Presidents -Survey-for-Education-Counsel-2.pdf.

3. "CASE 10-Cubed," YouTube video, 11:07, posted by "CASE Advance," February 16, 2018, https://www.youtube.com/watch?v=gmvJZKvpQ5M.

4. "CASE 10-Cubed."

5. Chronicle Insights Group, "Higher Ed Marketing Comes of Age: Data and Insights from College Marketing Leaders" (Washington, DC: Chronicle of Higher Education, 2014), 26, http://results.chronicle.com /CMOAMA.

6. Anna Myers, Susannah Baker, Helen Carasso, and Jennifer Gunthart, *Distinctiveness in Higher Education* (Oxford: Oxford Brookes University, 2016), 4.

7. John Pulley, "Romancing the Brand," *Chronicle of Higher Education*, October 24, 2003, https://www.chronicle.com/article/Romancing-the -Brand/2712.

8. Nathan D. Grawe, *Demographics and the Demand for Higher Education* (Baltimore: Johns Hopkins University Press, 2018).

9. Robert Zemsky, Susan Shaman, and Susan Campbell Baldridge, *The College Stress Test: Tracking Institutional Futures across a Crowded Market* (Baltimore: Johns Hopkins University Press, 2020).

10. See Lee Gardner, "On-line Protests Give New Arizona State U Mascot a Devil of a Time," *Chronicle of Higher Education*, March 12, 2013,

https://www.chronicle.com/blogs/bottomline/online-protests-give
-new-arizona-state-u-mascot-a-devil-of-a-time/; Xarissa Holdaway,
"Many People Still Hate the New U. of California Logo," *Chronicle of
Higher Education*, December 12, 2012, https://www.chronicle.com
/blogs/ticker/many-people-still-hate-the-new-u-of-california-logo
/52933; and Don Troop, "Did Drake's Ad Campaign Give Itself a Near
Failing Grade?," *Chronicle of Higher Education*, September 2, 2010,
https://www.chronicle.com/blogs/tweed/did-drakes-ad-campaign
-give-itself-a-near-failing-grade/26672.

11. Karl Einolf, interview by author, August 28, 2019.
12. Elizabeth Johnson, interview by author, August 13, 2019.
13. Troy Hammond, interview by author, September 27, 2019.
14. Margaret L. Drugovich, interview by author, September 10, 2019.
15. Einolf interview.
16. Einolf interview.
17. "Lipman Hearne. A Great Strategy Tells a Great Story: AKA's New
    Alliance," AKA Strategy, accessed September 20, 2019, https://
    akastrategy.com/affiliates-lipman-hearne/.
18. Bill Faust, interview by author, September 3, 2019.

Chapter 1. The Basics

1. Larry Litten, Daniel Sullivan, and David Brodigan, *Applying Research
   in College Admissions* (New York: College Entrance Examination Board,
   1983), 148.
2. Robert Sevier, *Integrated Marketing for Colleges, Universities, and Schools:
   A Step-by-Step Planning Guide* (Washington, DC: CASE, 1998), 29.
3. Philip Kotler, *Marketing for Nonprofit Organizations* (Englewood Cliffs,
   NJ: Prentice-Hall, 1975), 5.
4. Sevier, *Integrated Marketing*, 30.
5. Jerome E. McCarthey, *Basic Marketing: A Managerial Approach* (Home-
   wood, IL: R. D. Irwin, 1960).
6. Litten, Sullivan, and Brodigan, *Applying Research in College Admissions*,
   247.
7. Litten, Sullivan, and Brodigan, *Applying Research in College Admissions*, 15.
8. Litten, Sullivan, and Brodigan, *Applying Research in College Admissions*,
   247.
9. Thomas Hayes, *Marketing Colleges and Universities: A Services Approach*
   (Washington, DC: CASE, 2009).

10. Harvey Golub, Jane Henry, John L. Forbis, Nitin T. Mehta, Michael J. Lanning, Edward G. Michaels, and Kenichi Ohmae, "Delivering Value to Customers," *McKinsey Quarterly*, June 2000, https://www.mckinsey.com/business-functions/strategy-and-corporate-finance/our-insights/delivering-value-to-customers.

11. "Number of degree-granting postsecondary institutions and enrollment in these institutions, by enrollment size, control, and classification of institution: Fall 2017," National Center for Education Statistics, https://nces.ed.gov/programs/digest/d18/tables/dt18_317.40.asp.

12. Susannah Baker and Anna Meyers, *The Challenge of Being Distinctive: What You Stand For and How It Delivers Strategic Advantage* (Washington, DC: CASE, 2017).

13. Andrea Naddaff, quoted in John Pulley, "Romancing the Brand," *Chronicle of Higher Education*, October 24, 2003, https://www.chronicle.com/article/Romancing-the-Brand/2712.

14. Philip Kotler and Karen F. A. Fox, *Strategic Marketing for Educational Institutions* (Englewood Cliffs, NJ: Prentice-Hall, 1985); Kevin Lane Keller, *Strategic Brand Management* (Upper Saddle River, NJ: Prentice-Hall, 1998).

15. Keller, *Strategic Brand Management*.

16. Kotler and Fox, *Strategic Marketing for Educational Institutions*.

Chapter 2. Getting Started or Starting Fresh

1. Philip Kotler, "Strategies for Introducing Marketing in Nonprofit Organizations," *Journal of Marketing* 43, no. 1 (January 1979): 41.

2. Thomas Hayes, *Marketing Colleges and Universities: A Services Approach* (Washington, DC: CASE, 2009), 83.

3. Hayes, *Marketing Colleges and Universities*, 82.

4. Larry D. Lauer, *The Transition Academy: Seizing Opportunity in the Age of Disruption* (Washington, DC: CASE, 2016), 106.

5. Andrew Paradise, "Findings from the 2015 CASE Educational Communications and Marketing Trends Survey," CASE White Paper (Washington, DC.: CASE, 2017), https://www.case.org/resources/findings-2015-case-educational-communications-and-marketing-trends-survey-0.

6. Emily Glazer and Melissa Korn, "Marketing Pros: Big Brand on Campus," *Wall Street Journal*, August 15, 2012, https://www.wsj.com/articles/SB10000872396390444233104577591171686709792.

7. Kimberly Whitler, "Why Higher Education Institutions Need CMOs," *Forbes*, June 4, 2015, https://www.forbes.com/sites/kimberlywhitler/2015/06/04/why-higher-education-institutions-need-cmos/#1c5042b02025.

8. Hayes, *Marketing Colleges and Universities*, 87.

9. Paradise, "2015 CASE Trends Survey."

10. SimpsonScarborough, "The 2019 State of Higher Ed Marketing," 2019, simpsonscarborough.com/CMOStudy; Chronicle Insights Group, "Higher Ed Marketing Comes of Age: Data and Insights from College Marketing Leaders" (Washington, DC: Chronicle of Higher Education, 2014), http://results.chronicle.com/CMOAMA.

11. Chronicle Insights Group, "Higher Ed Marketing Comes of Age."

12. Andrew Paradise, Rae Goldsmith, Doug Goldenberg-Hart, and Judith Kroll, "From Evolution to Revolution: Findings from the Inaugural CASE Educational Communications and Marketing Trends Survey," CASE White Paper (Washington, DC: CASE 2015), https://www.case.org/resources/evolution-revolution-findings-inaugural-case-educational-communications-and-marketing-0.

13. SimpsonScarborough, "2019 State of Higher Ed Marketing."

14. Chronicle Insights Group, "Higher Ed Marketing Comes of Age"; Paradise, "2015 CASE Trends Survey"; SimpsonScarborough, "2019 State of Higher Ed Marketing."

15. Angela Polec, "The Role of the Chief Marketing Officer in Higher Education: Leveraging Bureaucratic and Network Power to Effect Change" (EdD diss., University of Pennsylvania, 2019), ProQuest (AAT 13902338).

16. Lauer, *Transition Academy*, 106.

17. Robert Sevier, *Integrated Marketing for Colleges, Universities, and Schools: A Step-by-Step Planning Guide* (Washington, DC: CASE, 1998), 108.

18. Sevier, *Integrated Marketing*, 109.

19. Glazer and Korn, "Marketing Pros."

20. Polec, "Role of Chief Marketing Officer."

21. Hayes, *Marketing Colleges and Universities*, 83.

22. See "We Know Success," American University, https://www.american.edu/weknowsuccess/.

23. Polec, "Role of Chief Marketing Officer."

24. Polec, "Role of Chief Marketing Officer," 180.

25. Polec, "Role of Chief Marketing Officer." See also Lee G. Bolman and Terrence E. Deal, *Reframing Organizations: Artistry, Choice, and Leader-*

ship, 3rd ed. (San Francisco: Jossey-Bass, 2003); and Omar Merlo, "The Influence of Marketing from a Power Perspective," *European Journal of Marketing* 45 (2011): 1152–71, doi:10.1108/03090561111113765130. Bureaucratic power is the formal power granted to the position based on structure and organizational context, reporting structure within the organization, and the components of the position's portfolio.

26. Polec, "Role of Chief Marketing Officer."
27. Chronicle Insights Group, "Higher Ed Marketing Comes of Age."
28. Paradise, "2015 CASE Trends Survey."
29. Lauer, *Transition Academy*, 105.
30. Chronicle Insights Group, "Higher Ed Marketing Comes of Age," 23.
31. SimpsonScaroborough, "2019 State of Higher Ed Marketing," 21.
32. Chronicle Insights Group, "Higher Ed Marketing Comes of Age," 24.
33. Paradise, "2015 CASE Trends Survey."
34. Polec, "Role of Chief Marketing Officer," 195, 124.
35. Chronicle Insights Group, "Higher Ed Marketing Comes of Age"; SimpsonScarborough, "2019 State of Higher Ed Marketing."
36. SimpsonScarborough, "2019 State of Higher Ed Marketing," 24.
37. Elizabeth Johnson, quoted in Piet Levy, "Class in Progress," *Marketing News*, November 5, 2009, 18, http://www.hiceschool.com/wp/wp-content/uploads/2009/12/BestinClass-Purdue.pdf.
38. Chronicle Insights Group, "Higher Ed Marketing Comes of Age," 8.
39. Chronicle Insights Group, "Higher Ed Marketing Comes of Age."
40. SimpsonScarborough, "2019 State of Higher Ed Marketing," 28.
41. SimpsonScarborough, "2019 State of Higher Ed Marketing," 11.
42. Paradise, "2015 CASE Trends Survey,"13.
43. Chronicle Insights Group, "Higher Ed Marketing Comes of Age," 8.
44. Lauer, *Transition Academy*.
45. Polec, "Role of Chief Marketing Officer."
46. SimpsonScarborough, "2019 State of Higher Ed Marketing," 29.
47. See Chronicle Insights Group, "Higher Ed Marketing Comes of Age"; and SimpsonScarborough, "2019 State of Higher Ed Marketing."
48. Council for the Advancement of Education Support, "Management Checklist for Communications and Marketing," https://www.case.org/system/files/media/file/Management%20Checklists%20for%20Communications%20and%20Marketing.pdf.
49. The Registry for College and University Presidents, https://www.registryinterim.com/.

Chapter 3. The Foundation

1. Robert Sevier, *Integrated Marketing for Colleges, Universities, and Schools: A Step-by-Step Planning Guide* (Washington, DC: CASE, 1998), 47.
2. Thomas Hayes, *Marketing Colleges and Universities: A Services Approach* (Washington, DC: CASE, 2009), 89.
3. Sevier, *Integrated Marketing*, 47.
4. Hayes, *Marketing Colleges and Universities*, 89–90.
5. Sevier, *Integrated Marketing*.
6. Sevier, *Integrated Marketing*, 47.
7. Elizabeth Johnson, interview by author, August 13, 2019. All quotations below are from this interview.

Chapter 4. What's the Big Idea?

1. Susannah Baker and Anna Meyers, *The Challenge of Being Distinctive: What You Stand For and How It Delivers Strategic Advantage* (Washington, DC: CASE, 2017).
2. Troy Hammond, interview by author, September 27, 2019.
3. "Who We Are," American University, accessed September 20, 2019, https://www.american.edu/about/history.cfm.
4. Bill Faust, interview by author, September 3, 2019; Peter Valdes-Dapena, "Volvo Promises Deathproof Cars by 2020," *CNN Business*, January 21, 2016, https://money.cnn.com/2016/01/20/luxury/volvo-no-death-crash-cars-2020/index.html.
5. Robert M. Moore, *The Real U: Building Brands That Resonate with Students, Faculty, Staff, and Donors* (Washington, DC: CASE, 2010), 52.
6. Moore, *Real U*, 53.
7. Moore, *Real U*, 58.
8. Hammond interview.
9. Elizabeth Johnson, interview by author, August 27, 2019.
10. Johnson interview.
11. Johnson interview.
12. Faust interview.
13. Faust interview.
14. Faust interview.
15. Faust interview.
16. Karl Einolf, interview by author, August 28, 2019.
17. Johnson interview; SimpsonScarborough, "The 2019 State of Higher Ed Marketing," 2019, simpsonscarborough.com/CMOStudy.

18. Jim Iovino, "Maryland Students Fear New University Slogan," *NBC Washington*, October 15, 2009, https://www.nbcwashington.com/news/sports/UMd-Students-Fear-New-School-Slogan-64397137.html; Ben Broman, "School Considering Dropping 'Fear the Turtle,'" *Testudo Times*, May 9, 2009, https://www.testudotimes.com/2009/5/9/870290/school-considering-dropping-fear; Nick Anderson, "U-Md. Marketing Evolves from 'Fear the Turtle' to 'Fearless Ideas,'" *Washington Post*, April 7, 2014, https://www.washingtonpost.com/local/education/u-md-marketing-evolves-from-fear-the-turtle-to-fearless-ideas/2014/04/07/ac857d36-be53-11e3-bcec-b71ee10e9bc3_story.html.

19. Max Foley-Keene, "UMD's Affinity for Pepsi and Amazon is Just Embarrassing," *Diamondback*, September 6, 2019, https://dbknews.com/2019/09/06/umd-amazon-pepsi-hq2-discovery-center/.

20. Faust interview; Hammond interview.

21. Johnson interview; Faust interview; Hammond interview.

22. Einolf interview; Faust interview; Hammond interview.

23. Hammond interview; Einolf interview.

24. Moore, *Real U*.

25. Faust interview.

26. Johnson interview.

27. Hammond interview.

Chapter 5. Integration of the Brand across the Institution

1. Doug Lederman, "A Graduate Program's Twist on Alternative Financing," *Inside Higher Ed*, September 13, 2019, https://www.insidehighered.com/digital-learning/article/2019/09/13/online-graduate-program-will-defer-half-tuition-charge-no.

2. "Experience AUx," American University, accessed September 16, 2019, https://www.american.edu/provost/undergrad/auexperience/.

3. Emily Canal, "The New Billion-Dollar Reason Why Northern Virginia Will Be the Next Tech Startup Hot Spot," *Inc.*, June 12, 2019, https://www.inc.com/emily-canal/virginia-tech-innovation-campus-amazon-hq2-northern-virginia.html.

4. Adam Harris, "What Johns Hopkins Gets By Buying the Newseum," *Atlantic*, January 25, 2019, https://www.theatlantic.com/education/archive/2019/01/johns-hopkins-purchase-newseum/581341/.

5. Michael Eicher, personal communication with author, September 9, 2019.

6. Larry D. Lauer, *The Transition Academy: Seizing Opportunity in the Age of Disruption* (Washington, DC: CASE, 2016), 113.
7. Lauer, *Transition Academy*.
8. Angela Polec, "The Role of the Chief Marketing Officer in Higher Education: Leveraging Bureaucratic and Network Power to Effect Change" (EdD diss., University of Pennsylvania, 2019), ProQuest (AAT 13902338).
9. "Brand Architecture," NC State University, accessed September 18, 2019, https://brand.ncsu.edu/architecture/.
10. "NC State Brand," NC State University, accessed September 18, 2019, https://brand.ncsu.edu.
11. "University of Buffalo: Identity and Brand—UB Message Map," University of Buffalo, accessed September 18, 2019, buffalo.edu /content/www/brand/strategy/ub-message-map.html; "University of Buffalo: How to Craft Our Story," University of Buffalo, accessed September 18, 2019, http://www.buffalo.edu/content/dam/www /brand/resources/Graduate%20and%20Professional%20Communica tions%20Guide%20FINAL%20May%202018.pdf.
12. Carrie Hane, "How to Improve Your Content Strategy Maturity, Part 1," *Content Science Review*, August 20, 2019, https://review.content-science .com/2019/08/how-to-improve-your-content-strategy-maturity-part-1/#.
13. Bill Walker, interview by author, September 20, 2019.

Chapter 6. Digital U

1. Jason Simon, "What Higher Ed Marketers Can Learn from Peloton (and Aviation Gin)," Thought Leadership, SimpsonScarborough, January 22, 2020, https://insights.simpsonscarborough.com/what -higher-ed-marketers-can-learn-from-peloton-and-aviation-gin.
2. Bob Hoffman, "The Problem With Bubba's Burgers," *Ad Contrarian Newsletter*, November 24, 2019, https://typeagroup.cmail20.com/t /ViewEmail/d/FFB570DBBAE6A23A2540EF23F30FEDED/C5DDCAA 278CE8CE3DBC23BD704D2542D.
3. Simon, "What Higher Ed Marketers Can Learn from Peloton."
4. Simon, "What Higher Ed Marketers Can Learn from Peloton."
5. Kevin Cary, "The Creeping Capitalist Takeover of Higher Education," Huffington Post, April 1, 2019, https://www.huffpost.com/highline /article/capitalist-takeover-college/.

6. Gartner, "Gartner Says Marketing Budgets Have Dropped Below 11% of Company Revenue for First Time Since 2014," Gartner, October 1, 2019, https://www.gartner.com/en/newsroom/press-releases/2019-10-01-gartner-says-marketing-budgets-have-dropped-below-11-.

7. Carrie Hane, "How to Improve Your Content Strategy Maturity, Part 1," *Content Science Review*, August 20, 2019, https://review.content-science.com/2019/08/how-to-improve-your-content-strategy-maturity-part-1/.

8. Tim Jones, "Be More Than Coordinated: Implementing Integrated Marketing at Beloit College," *Content Science Review*, March 20, 2018, https://review.content-science.com/2018/03/integrated-marketing-at-beloit-college/.

9. Jones, "Be More Than Coordinated."

10. Hane, "Content Strategy Maturity."

11. Jones, "Be More Than Coordinated."

12. Julia Zito, interview by author, September 30, 2019.

Chapter 7. Measuring Results and Progress

1. Anurag Harsh, "Five Steps to Change the Perception of Your Brand," *Forbes*, June 3, 2016, https://www.forbes.com/sites/forbesagencycouncil/2016/06/03/five-steps-to-change-the-perception-of-your-brand/#234f03ec6254.

2. Susannah Baker and Anna Myers, *The Challenge of Being Distinctive: What You Stand For and How It Delivers Strategic Advantage* (Washington, DC: CASE, 2017), 138.

3. Robert M. Moore and Tom Abrahamson, *Net Proceeds: Increased Revenue from Enrollment & Advancement—Guaranteed!* (Washington, DC: CASE, 2013), 7-25, quotation on 21.

4. Robert Sevier, *Integrated Marketing for Colleges, Universities, and Schools: A Step-by-Step Planning Guide* (Washington DC: CASE, 1998), 163.

5. Alumni Engagement Metrics Task Force, "Alumni Engagement Metrics," CASE White Paper (Washington, DC: CASE, 2018), https://www.case.org/system/files/media/file/CASEWhitePaper_Alumni Metrics%20AUG18.pdf.; "CASE Global Alumni Engagement Metrics Survey, 2019, Guidance Documentation" (Washington, DC: CASE, 2019), https://www.case.org/system/files/media/inline/CASE%20Alumni %20Engagement%20Metrics%20-%20Guidance%20Documentation%20 2019-08-29.pdf.

6. See "CIRP Freshman Survey," Higher Education Research Institute, University of California Los Angeles, https://heri.ucla.edu/cirp-freshman-survey/.

7. Richard Taylor, "Knowledge and Favourability," in Baker and Myers, *Challenge of Being Distinctive*, 116.

8. Taylor, "Knowledge and Favourability," 117–18.

9. "Measuring Your Net Promoter® Score," Bain & Company, https://www.netpromotersystem.com/about/measuring-your-net-promoter-score/.

10. Sevier, *Integrated Marketing*, 164.

11. Moore and Abrahamson, *Net Proceeds*, 21–23.

12. Karl Einolf, personal communication with author, April 19, 2020.

13. Karl Einolf, interview by author, August 28, 2019.

Chapter 8. Marketing Investment and Return on Investment

1. Nathan D. Grawe, *Demographics and the Demand for Higher Education* (Baltimore: Johns Hopkins University Press, 2018).

2. Lindsay McKenzie, "How Marketing Helped Southern New Hampshire University Make It Big Online," *Inside Higher Ed*, October 8, 2019, https://www.insidehighered.com/news/2019/10/08/how-marketing-helped-southern-new-hampshire-university-make-it-big-online.

3. Sarah Steimer, "CMO Survey: Hiring, AI on the Rise," *Marketing News* 53, no. 9 (October 2019): 6–7, https://www.ama.org/marketing-news/august-2019-cmo-survey-hiring-ai-on-the-rise/.

4. Kevin Carey, "The Creeping Capitalist Takeover of Higher Education," Huffington Post, April 1, 2019, https://www.huffpost.com/highline/article/capitalist-takeover-college/.

5. SimpsonScarborough, "The 2019 State of Higher Ed Marketing," 2019, simpsonscarborough.com/CMO Study, 16.

6. SimpsonScarborough, "2019 State of Higher Ed Marketing," 18.

7. Christine Moorman, "Marketing Budgets Vary by Industry," *CMO Today* (blog), *Wall Street Journal*, January 24, 2017, https://deloitte.wsj.com/cmo/2017/01/24/who-has-the-biggest-marketing-budgets/.

8. Carey, "Creeping Capitalist Takeover"; McKenzie, "How Marketing Helped Southern New Hampshire."

9. Chronicle Insights Group, "Higher Ed Marketing Comes of Age: Data and Insights from College Marketing Leaders" (Washington, DC:

Chronicle of Higher Education, 2014), http://results.chronicle.com
/CMOAMA; SimpsonScarborough "2019 State of Higher Education
Marketing."

10. SimpsonScarborough, "2019 State of Higher Ed Marketing," 31.
11. McKenzie, "How Marketing Helped Southern New Hampshire."
12. McKenzie, "How Marketing Helped Southern New Hampshire."
13. McKenzie, "How Marketing Helped Southern New Hampshire."
14. McKenzie, "How Marketing Helped Southern New Hampshire."
15. See Robert M. Moore and Tom Abrahamson, *Net Proceeds: Increased Revenue from Enrollment & Advancement—Guaranteed!* (Washington, DC: CASE, 2013), 17.
16. Moore and Abrahamson, *Net Proceeds*, 106.
17. Moore and Abrahamson, *Net Proceeds*, 107 (equation), 108.
18. Adam Hayes, "Brand Equity," Investopedia, May 3, 2019, https://www.investopedia.com/terms/b/brandequity.asp.
19. David Aaker, "What Is Brand Equity?," Prophet, September 4, 2013, https://www.prophet.com/2013/09/156-what-is-brand-equity-and-why-is-it-valuable/.

Chapter 9. The Future of Higher Education Marketing

1. Nathan D. Grawe, *Demographics and the Demand for Higher Education* (Baltimore: Johns Hopkins University Press, 2018), 4.
2. Grawe, *Demand for Higher Education*, 3.
3. See Hallie Busta, "Colleges just got a lot more leeway to recruit students," Education Dive, September 30, 2019, https://www.educationdive.com/news/colleges-just-got-a-lot-more-leeway-to-recruit-students/564016/.
4. Nathan Grawe, "Make the Most of a Natural Experiment," in "How Will the Pandemic Change Higher Education?," *Chronicle of Higher Education*, April 10, 2020, https://www.chronicle.com/article/How-Will-the-Pandemic-Change/248474.
5. Scott Carlson, "How Real-World Learning Could Help People Compete with Machines," *Chronicle of Higher Education*, November 20, 2017, https://www.chronicle.com/article/How-Real-World-Learning-Could/241811?cid=cp108; Joseph E. Aoun, "Robot-Proof: How Colleges Can Keep People Relevant in the Workplace," *Chronicle of Higher Education*, January 27, 2016, chronicle.com/article/Robot-Proof-How-Colleges-Can/235057.

6. Sarah Steimer, "CMO Survey: Hiring, AI on the Rise," *Marketing News* 53, no. 9 (October 2019): 6–7, https://www.ama.org/marketing-news /august-2019-cmo-survey-hiring-ai-on-the-rise/.

7. Steimer, "CMO Survey," 7.

8. US General Services Administration, "Eight Principles of Mobile-Friendliness: Don't Forget Accessibility!," Digital.gov, last modified March 7, 2019, https://digital.gov/resources/mobile/principles /accessibility/.

9. Zach Church, "Platform strategy, explained," MIT Management Sloan School, June 16, 2017, https://mitsloan.mit.edu/ideas-made-to-matter /platform-strategy-explained.

Index

awareness: of brand expression, 176-79; of brand strategy, 135; digital marketing for, 147-48; investments for, 192-93; measurement, 168, 169, 171, 172-76, 179, 181-82; among target audiences, 173-76, 181

best practices, 139-40
Big Idea, 102, 103
board, members: brand development and expression, 97, 103-4, 116; brand research, 76; consultant selection, 53, 79; investment, 196; marketing, 9-12, 14; roles, 4
brainstorming, 107, 109
brand: definition, 32-33; effective, 96; extended, 135; refinement, 117-19; strength, 33, 34; sustainability, 100
brand architecture, 134-35
brand development (platform), 95-106, 212; brand expression changes and, 117-19; design requirements, 96-100, 109; internal and external audiences, 100, 101; key pillars, 97-99; mistakes to avoid, 119-22; positioning statements, 84-85; roles and responsibilities for, 116; rubric, 100-106; stakeholders' vetting, 114-15
brand equity, 1, 7, 118, 119, 120, 131-32, 202-3; model, 33-34, 35
brand expression, 107-23; awareness of, 176-79; brand integration and, 135; changes, 117-19, 180-81, 183; choice of concept, 109-11; creative teams, 107-9; creative testing, 111-13; mistakes to avoid, 119-22; roles and responsibilities for, 116

branding, 45; definition, 33-34; indicators of effectiveness, 122-23; responsibility for, 58
brand loyalty, 10-11, 33, 34, 168, 169, 175
brand marketing impact measurement. *See* performance measures, of brand marketing
brand-name recognition, 6-7
brand research, 94, 102-3, 119-20; evaluation and distribution of findings, 87-88; financial resources, 85-87; goals, 90; internal and external audiences, 90; internal and external experts, 76-79; mistakes to avoid, 88-91; qualitative measures, 83, 84-85; quantitative measures, 83-85; replication, 91, 179-80, 181-82; scope of work, 81-87; time factors, 85-87
brand strategy, 31-32, 35; alignment with institutional strategy, 12-17, 117, 119-20, 128; alignment with strategic planning, 35; assessment, 182; changes, 117, 121-22, 182-83; content strategy alignment, 159-60; implementation, 113, 115-16, 124; stakeholders' vetting of, 113-15; timing, 12-17
brand strategy-related market research. *See* brand research
bridge-mirror positioning, 30-31, 84-85, 137
budget/expenditures, for marketing, 186-204, 213; benchmarking, 188-89, 190-92, 212-13; future of, 208; by institutional type, 189-90, 192, 196, 198; marketing effectiveness relationship, 193; media coverage, 194-96; as percentage of annual budget,

enterprise-level technologies (martech), 138-39, 208, 210

European Union, General Data Protection regulation, 146-47

executive leadership teams, 75, 88; CMO as member, 13-14, 45, 47, 50, 213

Facebook, 212

faculty: brand development role, 97, 104-5; brand research role, 80-81, 83-84, 86; support for marketing strategy, 8-9

familiarity, 81, 84, 112, 174, 179, 181

favorability, 84, 168, 175, 179, 181-82

"Fear the Turtle" campaign, 98, 100, 106, 119, 180-81, 196, 197

financial management, 9

financial status, effect of marketing on, 175-76

financial stress, 214

focus groups, 83, 84, 111-13

funding, 7

future, of marketing in higher education, 205-15; business strategy and, 212; content strategy, 210-11; data analytics in, 210; demographic changes, 6, 186-87, 203, 205-8, 214; impact of automation on, 208-10; technology's effects on workforce, 208-10

goals, of marketing, 6, 7, 8-9, 17-18, 203; financial status improvement, 175-76; identity distinction, 5; market research and, 94; performance metrics, 170; progress toward, 179; values exchange process and, 21

Google, 144, 150-51, 194, 211

Google Analytics, 155

government relations, 130

higher education, challenges to, 2

identity, institutional, 10-11

inclusiveness, of brand development and expression, 120, 122-23, 124, 134

Inside Higher Ed, 188

Instagram, 144

institutional research office, 77

institutional strategy, alignment with brand strategy, 12-17, 117, 119-20, 128

Integrated Postsecondary Education Data System (IPDES), 92

integration, of the brand strategy, 124-40; audience segmentation, 136; content strategy, 137-38; enterprise-level technologies, 138-39; integrated marketing communication, 128-33; leadership, 139-40; place decisions, 126-28; pricing decisions, 125-26; product decisions, 126; tools for, 133-39

internal capacity, for marketing and communication. *See* organizational capacity/ structure

international students, 2

interviews, 83, 84-85, 86, 104, 105, 173

investments, in marketing. *See* budget/expenditures, for marketing

IPEDS (Integrated Postsecondary Education Data System), 92

Keller's brand equity model, 33-34, 35

leadership, of strategic communication and marketing function, 37-40; brand strategy integration,

online program managers (OPMs), 142, 150, 152-53; 2U, 149-50, 153

opinion leaders, 41, 63, 173-74

organizational capacity/structure, 37; assessment, 66-68; benchmark data, 54, 56; bureaucratic power, 61-62; centralized *vs.* decentralized, 51-52, 57-60; marketing task force, 62-64; responsibilities, 57-62; size, 54-56; steering committees, 62, 65; structural complexity, 56-66; working groups, 62, 64-65

outsourcing, 51, 52-53, 56, 58-59, 109, 142; digital marketing, 152, 153, 154

parents, 4, 8, 10, 71, 86, 90, 130, 146, 174, 177, 182

partners/partnerships, 1, 18, 40, 51, 61, 134, 164, 169, 171, 186; agency partners, 52-53, 141, 142, 159; between business and academic institutions, 28, 126-27; information technology, 184; selection of, 52-53

peer assessment, 172-73

peer review, 8

performance measures, of brand marketing, 214; benchmarking, 212-13; dashboards, 171, 213; financial status, 175-76; long-term measures, 181-83; long-term measures baseline, 173-75; middle-term measures, 179-81, 182; ongoing measures baseline, 170-73; as proxy measures, 168-69, 171-73, 181; regular reporting of, 183-84; short-term measures, 176-79

philanthropy, 7, 20, 45, 46, 128

place decisions, 24-25, 49-50, 93, 126-28, 212

platform strategy. *See* brand development (platform)

positioning, as brand strategy component, 102

positioning statements, 25-32, 35, 84-85; stakeholder surveys, 105; targeted to audience segments, 136-37; three Rs, 31

presidents: as brand champions, 133; brand development and expression role, 116; brand research role, 76, 88; brand vetting role, 113-14; perspectives on marketing, 4-7; relationship with CMO, 45, 47

price decisions, 21, 24, 35, 49-50, 91-92, 93, 125-26

price elasticity, 33, 49, 91

priorities, institutional, 96

product decisions, 24, 35, 49-50, 93, 126

product marketing, 23, 24

professional organizations, content strategy, 158

professional schools, brand strategy integration, 131

promotion decisions, 6, 8, 20, 21, 24, 25, 93

provosts, 3, 7-9, 17, 51-52, 104, 139

public relations and media strategy, 45, 47, 58, 130

public service announcements (PSAs), 5-6

quality: as brand strategy component, 97, 98; customers' perceptions, 34, 38, 165, 168, 181-82, 203, 210; marketing return on investment and, 194-95, 198; tuition as indicator, 91-92

quality control, 161-62

rankings, academic, 8, 9, 172-73
The Real U: Building Brands That Resonate with Students, Faculty, Staff, and Donors, 102
recruitment: future trends, 207; performance measures, 170. *See also* enrollment
recruitment, digital strategies. *See* digital marketing
Reddit, 144
regional differentiation, 30
Registry for College and University Presidents, 68
relevance, 2, 8, 31, 84, 100, 109, 116, 126, 183; of content marketing, 149, 151, 159
reporting structures: CMOs, 45-48, 49, 50, 213; marketing and communication functions, 51, 53, 56-57
reputation, 1, 2, 7, 9; awareness of, 172-74, 175, 181-82; brand strength and, 33; incremental changes, 179; provosts' perspectives, 7-8; responsibility for maintenance, 58
research: funding, 41; marketing communication about, 130
research experts, 77, 78-80, 94
research support, performance measures, 170-71
research universities: differentiation, 105-6; positioning statements, 28-29
responsibilities, in marketing and communication function: levels, 57-62; for marketing expenditures, 199-200
responsibility-centered management (RCM), 131-32, 199-200
resumé commitment, 164-65
retention, 21, 49; curriculum and, 6-7; digital marketing-based,

142; financial return on, 214; future trends, 207; predictors, 56
return on investment (ROI), 184, 187-88, 194-95, 198-202; calculation, 199-202; cost of acquisition, 198-99, 200-201
revenue: lifetime value of students and alumni, 176; non-tuition sources, 13; percentage spent on marketing, 188

search engine marketing (SEM), 150-51
search engine optimization (SEO), 148-50, 151, 153, 155, 156, 157, 193
segmentation. *See* audience segments; market segments
services marketing, 23-25, 43-44
simplicity, 96, 97, 109, 111
Siri, 144
social media, 10-11, 113, 122, 137-38, 144, 147, 177
staff: brand development role, 97; brand research role, 80-81, 84; as creative team members, 108; in marketing and communication, 52, 54-56
stakeholders, 23; brand development and expression role, 111-13, 120, 121, 122; brand research role, 79-80, 81, 88-89, 90; brand vetting role, 113-15; engagement, 6, 7; loyalty, 10-11; as market target audience, 5, 6; relevance of brand to, 100, 101. *See also* alumni engagement; donors; faculty; parents; students
strategic integrated marketing, 11, 18, 31-32, 37, 39, 40, 45, 75; responsibilities in, 57, 60, 62
strategic planning, 4, 13, 35

student debt, 214
students: brand research role, 80-81, 86, 90; as digital marketing audience, 143-46; lifetime revenue value, 176, 199, 214; marketing task force membership, 63; targeted segments, 7; values exchange experience, 20-21
student satisfaction, 24
sub-brands, 135
surveys, 8, 24, 45, 54, 84, 87, 105, 173-74, 188; omnibus, 179-80; online, 81, 83; of public opinion, 179-80
sustainability, 28, 30, 100, 109, 111, 117

teacher certification, 149-50
three Rs (real, rare, and relevant), 31, 96
trademarks, 63, 135
transparency, 49, 88, 178, 183, 196, 198
tuition, 24, 49; marketing expenditures and, 196, 198; pricing decisions, 91-92, 125-26; resets, 6-7; revenue diversification, 6; as values exchange, 20-21
two-year colleges, 206-7

University of California, Los Angeles, Higher Education Research Institute, 171
University of Maryland: brand development, 96, 97-98, 100, 105-6; brand expression, 119; "Fear the Turtle" campaign, 119, 180-81, 196, 197; as University of Maryland System flagship, 97;

"ZOOM" campaign, 98, 177-78, 180-81
US News & World Report, academic rankings, 8, 172

value(s), 4; distinguished from value propositions, 29; of higher education, 1, 214-15; in marketing context, 20, 186
value, exchanges of, 20-21, 20-24; brand strategy and, 35; brand strength and, 33, 34; customers in, 20, 21, 22, 23, 24; demand-side, 22; digital marketing and, 146; digital technology's impact on, 142-43; exchange side, 20-22; shared responsibilities for, 60; suppliers/providers in, 20, 21, 22, 23
value proposition, 23, 25-32, 35
vice presidents: CMOs as, 49; for marketing, 37-38, 46, 47, 101-2, 164-65; marketing role, 14, 38, 39, 46, 51-52
vision, 4, 16, 30

web content management system. *See* content management systems
websites, 144; chatbots, 145-46; content strategy, 137-38; cookies-based tracking on, 145, 146-47; mobile-friendly formats, 211; requests for information (RFI), 145-47, 149-50; student searches, 144-46
work, future of, 208-10
workforce, future skills requirements, 209

YouTube, 144